NEIL MUNRO & IAN STONE

Lead Beyond Limits

Empower, Inspire, Transform – A Guide for Visionary Entrepreneurs

Copyright © 2024 by Neil Munro & Ian Stone

©2024 by Neil Munro & Ian Stone. All rights reserved. No part of this publication may be reproduced, distributed, or transmitted in any form or by any means, including photocopying, recording, or other electronic or mechanical methods, without the prior written permission of the authors, except in the case of brief quotations embodied in critical reviews and certain other noncommercial uses permitted by copyright law.

The advice and strategies contained herein may not be suitable for your situation. The authors and publisher make no representations or warranties with respect to the accuracy or completeness of the contents of this book and specifically disclaim any implied warranties of merchantability or fitness for a particular purpose. There are no warranties which extend beyond the descriptions contained in this paragraph. No legal or financial advice is being given in this book.

The authors and publisher shall not be liable for any loss of profit or any other commercial damages, including but not limited to special, incidental, consequential, or other damages. As always, the advice of a competent legal, tax, accounting, or other professional should be sought.

First edition

Contents

IMPORTANT: READ THIS FIRST	iv
INTRODUCTION	viii
UNLEASHING YOUR INNER LEADER	1
BUILDING YOUR LEADERSHIP FOUNDATION	11
INSPIRING AND MOTIVATING TEAMS	22
STRATEGIC LEADERSHIP	33
THE POWER OF INFLUENCE	45
DEVELOPING LEADERSHIP SKILLS	57
LEADING HIGH-PERFORMANCE TEAMS	68
ETHICAL LEADERSHIP AND CORPORATE RESPONSIBILITY	80
OVERCOMING LEADERSHIP CHALLENGES	92
THE FUTURE OF LEADERSHIP	103
EMBRACING YOUR LEADERSHIP DESTINY	115

IMPORTANT: READ THIS FIRST

Hi, we're Neil Munro and Ian Stone, and we're grateful you've picked up this book. If you've ever felt the desire to lead but struggled with how to inspire effectively or turn your vision into reality, you're certainly not alone. This guide comes from our over two decades of experience running businesses from scratch, where we've witnessed firsthand the myths and challenges that often hold leaders back. This book is our response to those challenges, crafted to empower and enlighten visionary entrepreneurs like yourself.

Throughout our journey in the leadership space, we've learned that there are so many misconceptions and unanswered questions about practical leadership tools. That's why we've put together this book to help you. Whether you're launching a start-up or running an established business, strong and effective leadership is a constant need across all stages and sizes of business.

Perhaps you've experienced the frustration of trying to communicate your vision, only to have it lost in translation, leaving your team unmotivated and your projects stalling. It's a common issue where the words you use don't quite capture the essence of your intentions.

You might also have battled with decision fatigue, feeling overwhelmed by the constant flow of choices and the pressure to always make the right call. It can be exhausting, particularly when each decision feels weightier than the last, draining your energy and clouding your judgment.

Or maybe you've felt the isolation that can come with leadership, where the corner office feels less like a position of power and more like a place of solitude.

It's not unusual for leaders to feel disconnected, struggling to maintain the personal connections that once fuelled their passion.

We get it—it's not fair.

The truth is, you're not alone. Many business owners and entrepreneurs are dealing with these exact challenges, facing waves of doubt and barriers to effective leadership.

That feeling of inadequacy, frustration, or even fear that you're not living up to your own expectations—or those of your peers—can be paralysing. It eats away at you, whispering that maybe you're not cut out for this, that perhaps you're out of your depth.

Here's what most people don't realise: these issues often stem not from a lack of desire or ability, but from a lack of clear, actionable strategies that resonate with both the leader and their team. Without these strategies, even the most passionate visionaries can find themselves adrift.

And as you look to expand into new markets or scale your operations, these leadership challenges can intensify, turning minor hurdles into major obstacles blocking your path to success.

This isn't just about business growth; it's about personal survival in the high-stakes world of entrepreneurship. Many are left in a constant state of self-doubt and worry, second-guessing every decision, fearing that one wrong move could undo all their hard work.

The Leadership Mirage

As visionary entrepreneurs, you may find yourself caught in a deceptive cycle that stifles your ability to lead effectively. This cycle, which we call The Leadership Mirage, traps many ambitious business owners in a loop of frustration. Let's break down each step of this cycle, which might resonate with your experiences.

Initiation of Insecurity

You may have felt that first twinge of doubt, questioning your leadership abilities. Perhaps it stemmed from a project that didn't go as planned or from feedback that wasn't as glowing as you expected. This insecurity triggers the cycle, pushing you to seek solutions, hoping to prove your capability.

Overcompensation Overdrive

In response to this self-doubt, you might have overcompensated—taking on more responsibilities, attending back-to-back seminars, reading every leadership book available. You want to prove to everyone—most of all, to yourself—that you can be that confident, effective leader. However, this overcompensation often leads to burnout, as the balance between personal life and leadership responsibilities tilts dangerously out of control.

Illusion of Achievement

As you power through your overextended commitments, there might be a fleeting moment of triumph. Maybe a successful deal or a brief surge in team morale makes you feel like you've finally cracked the code. But this illusion of achievement is short-lived, masking the deeper issues that haven't been resolved.

Reality Check

Inevitably, the cracks begin to show. A key team member might resign, or an important project could collapse unexpectedly. This reality check brings into sharp focus that the temporary high of the Illusion of Achievement wasn't a lasting solution. The foundation of your leadership, built on reactive measures rather than genuine growth, feels shaky once again.

Return to Insecurity

This step brings you full circle. The issues highlighted by the reality check reignite your original insecurities, making you feel as though despite your best efforts, you're no closer to becoming the leader you aspire to be. It's disheartening, and thus the cycle begins anew

It's clear that you need to adopt a different approach to become the confident, effective leaders who can inspire teams, overcome challenges, and drive success while maintaining a healthy personal and professional balance. This book will guide you to break free from this recurring pain and frustration.

We're glad you're reading this book because as you turn the pages, you will discover the insights and answers you've been searching for.

INTRODUCTION

Imagine standing on the precipice of your greatest potential. You, as an entrepreneur, are not just running a business; you're leading a charge towards innovation and success. In the ever-evolving landscape of global commerce, where each decision can pivot your company towards growth or reveal new challenges, how do you harness your inherent leadership skills to not only survive but thrive? Welcome to "Lead Beyond Limits: Empower, Inspire, Transform – A Guide for Visionary Entrepreneurs." This is where your journey transcends the ordinary and where you evolve to become the leader you were meant to be.

Empower Yourself to Empower Others

In the realm of business, leadership isn't merely a position; it's a performance in which you are constantly on stage. The spotlight is on you: your actions, your decisions, and most importantly, your ability to navigate through tempests while keeping your team focused and motivated. But before you can effectively lead others, you must first establish a profound and resilient connection with your inner leader. This isn't about external success alone; it's about tapping into your own values, visions, and virtues that drive your entrepreneurial spirit.

The leadership journey begins with self-awareness. Understanding your unique strengths and weaknesses is crucial. It's about aligning your personal mission with your business objectives, crafting a symbiotic relationship where each grows with the other. By empowering yourself, you set a precedent for your team. You become a beacon of strength and reliability, someone who not only directs but also participates in the quest for excellence.

Inspire Teams to Aspire

A leader's true might is measured not by personal accomplishments but by the success of their team. Inspiration is the fuel that powers your entrepreneurial engine. A truly visionary leader not only sets a clear vision but makes it compelling enough that others are naturally drawn to it. This magnetic pull is not achieved through authority but through authenticity, empathy, and by being genuinely invested in the welfare of those who follow you.

But how do you transform individual potential into collective success? It's about creating an environment that promotes innovation, where mistakes are seen as learning opportunities rather than failures. It's about encouraging your team to experiment, to question, and to take ownership of their roles. When a team feels trusted and valued, their motivation shifts from merely doing what is expected to excelling in their endeavours.

Transform Challenges into Opportunities

The path of leadership is fraught with challenges. However, every challenge carries the seeds of opportunity. In the dynamic world of business, adaptability is your greatest tool. Whether it's navigating through economic downturns, managing technological disruptions, or addressing market competition, your ability to pivot and persevere determines your business's resilience.

Transformative leadership involves foresight—the ability to anticipate and prepare for future challenges. It requires a balance between maintaining your core values and remaining agile in your strategies. This book will not only provide you with the insights to recognise potential pitfalls but also the strategies to turn these challenges into stepping stones for growth.

Why This Book?

"Lead Beyond Limits" isn't just another leadership manual; it's a manifesto for revolutionary leadership. You are already on the entrepreneurial path, making decisions daily that affect many lives. This guide is designed to refine your leadership style, amplify your influence, and help you forge a legacy of impactful, ethical, and sustainable business practices.

By reading this book, you equip yourself with more than just knowledge; you empower yourself with wisdom to lead not just effectively, but inspirationally. Whether you're at the helm of a startup or steering a large corporation, the principles contained within these pages are universal and transformative.

In conclusion, the essence of visionary entrepreneurial leadership lies in seeing beyond the immediate horizon, in believing in your ability to effect change and having the courage to take action. "Lead Beyond Limits" invites you to step into your power, to embrace your role as a leader fully, and to embark on a journey that promises personal growth, team success, and a lasting impact on the business landscape.

Welcome to a new chapter in your entrepreneurial journey.

Welcome to leadership that transcends boundaries and sets new benchmarks.

Welcome to your future.

UNLEASHING YOUR INNER LEADER

"The very essence of leadership is that you have to have a vision." – Theodore Hesburgh

Understanding Leadership

When you delve into the concept of leadership, particularly in the modern business environment, it's like peeling an onion. Each layer offers new insights, complexities, and sometimes even a few tears. As an entrepreneur, understanding these layers is not just beneficial—it's crucial for your growth and the growth of your business.

Defining Leadership in Modern Business

Leadership has evolved significantly over the decades. Gone are the days when being a leader simply meant holding a title and delegating tasks. Today, leadership in business transcends traditional boundaries and hierarchies. It's about inspiring and influencing others, regardless of your position or title.

In modern business, being a leader means being at the forefront of change. It involves not only managing and directing but also inspiring and empowering your team. You're expected to be a visionary, a strategist, a coach, and sometimes, even a friend. The role intertwines professional acumen with personal integrity and emotional intelligence.

For you, as an entrepreneur, leadership means embodying the ethos of your business. Your actions, decisions, and the culture you cultivate all reflect back on your understanding of what it means to lead. It's about making decisions that not only drive profitability but also foster a positive environment and promote sustainable practices.

Traits of Effective Leaders

Reflect on leaders you admire. What traits make them stand out? You might be thinking of qualities like charisma, intelligence, or perhaps decisiveness. While these are all important, effective leadership, especially in a fast-paced entrepreneurial context, requires a broader set of traits.

1. **Adaptability:** In today's fast-evolving market landscapes, the ability to pivot and adapt to changing circumstances is invaluable. You must be ready to face new challenges, alter your strategies, and sometimes, even overhaul your business model to stay relevant.

2. **Transparency:** This is about being open in your communication and honest about your business operations. It builds trust and respect among your team members and stakeholders, creating a loyal and supportive work environment.

3. **Empathy:** Understanding and sharing the feelings of another is crucial in today's business world. It helps in nurturing a supportive workplace, where personal growth and professional development are prioritised.

4. **Decisiveness:** Being able to make decisions swiftly and effectively, even under pressure, sets a leader apart. It's not just about making the most choices, but making the right ones.

5. **Visionary Thinking:** As a leader, you should see beyond the day-to-day operations and plan for the future. This involves setting goals that are ambitious yet achievable, and inspiring your team to strive towards these goals.

Incorporating these traits into your leadership style isn't about a radical transformation but fine-tuning your natural abilities and qualities in ways that align with your business ethos and the expectations of modern entrepreneurial ventures.

Different Leadership Styles

Understanding different leadership styles is like having various tools in your toolbox. Each tool can be effective depending on the situation. Here are a few styles that you might find resonate with your personal approach or could be useful in certain aspects of your business:

1. **Autocratic Leadership:** This style is characterized by individual control over all decisions with little input from group members. It can be useful in situations where fast decision-making is crucial.

2. **Democratic Leadership:** Contrary to the autocratic style, democratic leadership encourages the sharing of responsibilities and decision-making among group members. This can enhance team morale and creativity, leading to more sustainable business solutions.

3. **Transformational Leadership:** This style is all about initiating change in organizations, groups, and oneself. It's highly suited to businesses that are looking to reinvent or need to pivot their direction.

4. **Laissez-Faire Leadership:** A French phrase that translates literally as "let do," in this style, the rights and power to make decisions are delegated to the workforce. This can be effective in creative environments where individuals are motivated by autonomy.

5. **Situational Leadership:** Recognising that different situations require different kinds of leadership, this style suggests that leaders should adapt their approach to the specific needs of their team and project conditions.

Each of these styles has its merits and limitations. The key as an entrepreneurial leader is not to rigidly adhere to one style but to be flexible and adaptable, choosing the best approach based on the circumstances and the specific needs of your team and business goals.

Understanding leadership in the context of contemporary business is not just about mastering these definitions, traits, and styles. It's about realising that each element is part of a larger dynamic that influences how you lead and succeed. As you reflect on these concepts, consider not just how you can integrate them into your own leadership approach, but also how they can shape the future trajectory of your entrepreneurial journey.

Mindset of a Leader

Growth Mindset vs. Fixed Mindset

Imagine stepping into the arena of entrepreneurship where each decision, each failure, and each success fundamentally shapes your journey. The mindset you adopt as you navigate this journey can significantly influence your trajectory. Now, let's dissect two contrasting perspectives: the growth mindset and the fixed mindset.

With a fixed mindset, abilities are seen as static, inherent traits that one either has or doesn't. It's like being stuck in a mental room with unchangeable walls. This perspective can severely limit your potential because it roots you in the belief that your capabilities are set in stone—either you're born a leader, or you're not. If you encounter failure, it becomes a direct assault on your identity rather than an opportunity for growth.

Conversely, adopting a growth mindset transforms your approach. This mindset thrives on challenge and sees failure not as evidence of unintelligence but as a heartening springboard for growth and for stretching existing abilities. In this mindset, there's an underlying belief that your basic qualities are things you can cultivate through effort. Yes, people differ significantly in their initial talents and aptitudes, interests, or temperaments, but everyone can change and grow through application and experience.

As an entrepreneur, fostering a growth mindset could be your golden ticket. It allows you to learn from setbacks, then adapt and move forward. This adaptability is crucial in the fast-paced, ever-changing world of business. When you view challenges as opportunities to improve, your business is more likely to thrive and stand resilient in the face of adversity.

Importance of Resilience

Resilience is your business's shock absorber. It's the ability to bounce back from setbacks, adapt well to change, and keep going in the face of adversity. In the entrepreneurial world, resilience is what separates those who falter and fade away from those who flourish and forge ahead.

Building resilience is not just about getting through tough times but also how you react to them. It involves developing a set of attributes that allows you to remain focused, flexible, and productive, in bad times as well as good. The greater your reservoir of resilience, the more you can withstand the pressure.

Consider resilience as a skill, not a trait. It involves behaviours, thoughts, and actions that can be learned and developed by anyone. How do you foster this resilience? Start by maintaining a positive outlook and focusing on what you can control. When faced with a setback, instead of spiralling into despair, analyse the situation. What can be learned? How can this new knowledge be applied moving forward?

Moreover, don't underestimate the power of a support network. Surround yourself with advisers, mentors, and peers who can offer guidance and insights. Their experience and support can be crucial buffers against the rough-and-tumble realities of running a business.

Cultivating Emotional Intelligence

Emotional intelligence (EQ) is the unsung hero of effective leadership. It's your ability to recognise, understand, and manage not only your own emotions but also those of others. In leadership, having high emotional intelligence helps you manage stress better, deliver feedback effectively, and create a motivational environment for your team.

Firstly, self-awareness is key; it's about knowing your own emotions, strengths, weaknesses, drives, values, and goals – and their impact on others. As a leader, when you demonstrate self-awareness, you are better equipped to make informed decisions, communicate clearly, and foster trust and authenticity.

Then there's empathy, a powerful tool in your leadership arsenal. It allows you to understand and share the feelings of another, which can profoundly influence how you deal with conflicts and build relationships. Being empathetic shows your team that you value their input and care about their well-being, which can boost morale and loyalty.

Lastly, let's talk about self-regulation. This aspect of EQ involves controlling or redirecting your disruptive emotions and impulses and adapting to changing circumstances. Think of it as emotional agility - being able to recover quickly from emotional experiences and not letting setbacks derail your actions.

For entrepreneurs, cultivating emotional intelligence can lead to better business outcomes. It enhances your negotiations, improves your team's cohesion, and fosters a work environment that is conducive to high performance.

In sum, the mindset of a leader is about much more than just setting strategies or making decisions. It's about nurturing a growth mindset that welcomes challenges and learns from failures. It's about building resilience to weather the storms of entrepreneurship. And it's about developing emotional intelligence to effectively connect with, lead, and inspire your team. Embracing these elements can transform your leadership approach and set you on a path to not just meet but exceed your entrepreneurial goals.

Setting Your Vision

Crafting a compelling vision is essentially about dreaming big. It's about looking beyond the day-to-day operations and imagining where you want your enterprise to be in the future. This isn't just about setting targets or goals; it's about capturing an inspiring picture that will serve as a north star for you and your team.

Start by allowing yourself the freedom to dream without constraints. Think about the 'why' behind your business. Why did you start it? What change did you want to see in the world? Your vision should amplify this purpose. It needs to be bold, clear, and resonate on a personal level with everyone involved in the organisation.

Crafting this vision isn't a solo flight. Engage with your team, gather insights from them, and understand what drives them. This collaborative approach not only enriches the vision but also ensures it is shared widely, enhancing commitment across your organisation. Remember, a vision that is co-created is often more powerful and far-reaching.

Once your vision is clear, it's crucial to align it with your business goals. This is where many leaders falter; they either have a vision that's too abstract, lacking actionable steps, or they have concrete plans that don't inspire. The trick is to find a balance. Break down your vision into actionable and measurable goals.

Think of your vision as the destination and your business goals as the map that gets you there. Each goal should be a step that moves you closer to realising your vision. This alignment is crucial because it ensures that every aspect of your business is working towards the same endpoint. It's about making sure your daily operations support your long-term aspirations.

Communicating your vision effectively is the final piece of the puzzle. It's not enough to have a great vision; you must be able to share it in a way that excites and motivates others. Storytelling can be a powerful tool here. Narratives that illustrate the impact of achieving your vision can engage emotions and inspire action.

However, clarity is paramount. Your vision should be easily understandable, and anyone in your organisation should be able to articulate it. Regularly reinforce your vision through meetings, newsletters, or any internal communications. Make it a part of the everyday language of your business.

Remember, the way you communicate your vision can significantly influence its success. It should not only inform but also inspire your team, stakeholders, and even customers. Your enthusiasm and belief in the vision should be palpable in every interaction, setting the tone for others to follow.

In essence, setting your vision is about dreaming big, aligning strategically, and communicating passionately. This approach not only sets the direction for your business but also ignites an ongoing inspiration that can propel your team to achieve extraordinary results. As you embark on this journey, consider your vision not as a fixed point but as a guiding light, evolving as you and your business grow. Keep it at the forefront of all you do, and watch as it shapes your path to success.

RECAP AND ACTION ITEMS

You've just navigated through the essential terrains of leadership, mindset, and vision—three cornerstones of transformative leadership. Let's consolidate what you've learnt and turn these insights into actionable steps that will catapult you and your business into new heights.

Starting with the essence of leadership, you now understand that modern business demands a leader who is adaptable, insightful, and above all, effective in diverse environments. You've explored various leadership styles and identified the traits that resonate most with your personal and business ethos. The challenge now is to reflect on your current leadership approach and pinpoint areas for development. Ask yourself: Which traits do I already embody? Which areas need more attention? Set a plan to enhance those key leadership traits through specific actions, like seeking feedback from peers or enrolling in a relevant workshop.

Moving to the mindset of a leader, you've dissected the growth versus fixed mindset and the paramount importance of resilience and emotional intelligence. These are not just buzzwords; they are your armour in the entrepreneurial battlefield. To foster a growth mindset, start by re-framing failures as learning opportunities. Keep a journal of daily or weekly reflections to monitor your progress and setbacks, learning from each. For boosting resilience, challenge yourself regularly with new tasks that stretch your comfort zone slightly. And for emotional intelligence, practice mindfulness and active listening in your interactions—these skills will enhance your relationships both within and outside your business.

Finally, setting your vision has never been more critical. A compelling vision acts as the north star for you and your team. Take the vision you've crafted and break it down into actionable goals. Align these with the broader business objectives to ensure coherence and focus. Communicate this vision effectively and consistently, using stories and visuals that resonate with your team's values and aspirations.

Your action items? Define your leadership development areas, adopt a resilience-building challenge, enhance your emotional intelligence, and articulate your vision in ways that mobilise and inspire your team. Remember, the journey of a thousand miles begins with a single step. Take that step today, and start leading beyond limits.

BUILDING YOUR LEADERSHIP FOUNDATION

"Before you are a leader, success is all about growing yourself. When you become a leader, success is all about growing others." - Jack Welch

Core Values and Principles

Identifying Your Core Values

In the labyrinth of entrepreneurship, your core values are the Ariadne's thread that guides you through the complexities of decision-making, team building, and brand positioning. These aren't just placards to decorate the office walls; they are the bedrock on which your company stands. But how do you go about identifying these values?

Start by examining the moments when you felt most fulfilled in your work. What were you doing? Who were you helping? The patterns in these answers are goldmines. For example, if you constantly find satisfaction in innovation and problem-solving, 'innovation' might be a core value for your business.

Next, consider the traits that you admire in others, especially those you respect as leaders or competitors. These qualities often reflect the values that you, too, hold dear.

Once you've gathered a list, it's time to refine it. Aim for around five core values—too many and they lose their impact, too few and they might not cover the breadth of your business ethos. These should be clear and actionable. For instance, instead of 'good customer service', opt for 'empathy' or 'responsiveness', which suggest a more direct course of action.

How Principles Guide Leadership

With your core values defined, they can begin to inform your principles—the rules and guidelines that dictate how you and your team operate on a day-to-day basis. Think of your values as your destination and your principles as the roadmap that gets you there. They translate your values into practical, everyday behaviours that set the standard for your company's culture.

For instance, if one of your core values is 'integrity', your principles might include always being transparent about your business practices, or ensuring that all your products meet certain ethical standards before they hit the market.

These principles do more than just guide your own behaviour; they influence the actions of your entire team. When clearly communicated, they provide a framework that helps everyone make decisions that align with the heart of the company. This consistency is crucial not only for internal harmony but also for brand reliability in the eyes of your customers.

Leading by Example

The most potent way to cement these values and principles in your company culture is to embody them yourself. This is where 'leading by example' transitions from a cliché to a leadership imperative. The truth is, people believe what they see more than what they hear. If you're preaching punctuality but consistently showing up late to meetings, your words lose their weight.

Leading by example means being the first to adhere to the guidelines you've set out, whether that's maintaining open communication, pursuing continuous education, or showing respect to all team members. When challenges arise, your team will watch to see how you apply your values and principles to navigate the situation. This not only reinforces the behaviours you want to encourage but also builds trust and respect.

Moreover, this approach opens a genuine dialogue about why these values and principles matter. It's one thing to tell your team to value customer feedback, and quite another to show them by personally following up on a customer issue. These actions make the intangible tangible and demonstrate that your company's values are not just motivational posters but real standards that everyone, including you as the leader, is expected to live by.

By setting this example, you create a ripple effect throughout your organisation. Team members are more likely to emulate these behaviours, which reinforces the culture you're aiming to build. This doesn't just apply to higher-level management; it should permeate through every layer of your company. When each member of your team understands and shares in the vision and operates according to the same set of principles, your business's ability to make a real impact increases exponentially.

As you continue to lead, remember that your personal alignment with these core values and principles is not a one-time setup. It's a continuous journey of self-reflection and adjustment, ensuring that as your business evolves, your foundational values remain consistent and continue to guide your leadership style. This consistency is key not only to personal integrity but also to your business's long-term success and reputation. By fostering a culture that mirrors your deepest values, you empower your team, inspire your customers, and transform challenges into stepping stones. This is the essence of visionary leadership.

Decision-Making Skills

Frameworks for Effective Decision-Making

When faced with a decision, how do you proceed? Do you go with your gut, or do you have a tried and tested method? As a leader, the decisions you make can have far-reaching implications. Using a structured approach not only streamlines the process but also increases the likelihood of achieving favourable outcomes.

One popular framework is the DECIDE Model. This six-step process stands for Define the problem, Establish the criteria, Consider the alternatives, Identify the best alternative, Develop and implement a plan, and Evaluate and monitor the solution and feedback received. By breaking down decisions into these manageable steps, you can tackle even the most complex issues systematically.

Another effective strategy is the OODA Loop, used extensively in military strategy by the United States Air Force. It stands for Observe, Orient, Decide and Act. This model helps you to remain agile and adaptable, updating your approach as new information comes to light. This is particularly useful in fast-paced environments where conditions can change rapidly.

Utilising these frameworks, or others like the Pareto Analysis or the Cost-Benefit Analysis, provides you with a toolkit to approach decision-making with confidence. Experiment with different frameworks to find what best suits your style and your business's needs. Remember, the key is not just to make decisions but to make the right decisions consistently.

Balancing Risk and Reward

Risk is an inherent part of entrepreneurship. However, understanding and managing risk is what sets apart successful entrepreneurs from the rest. Balancing risk and reward is akin to walking a tightrope, where the goal is to reach the other side (success), without falling off (failure).

Firstly, assess the risk. What are the potential downsides? What could you lose? And importantly, what could you gain? Use tools like SWOT analysis (Strengths, Weaknesses, Opportunities, Threats) to get a clear picture of the potential risks and rewards.

Secondly, consider the risk-to-reward ratio. This involves comparing the potential gain from a decision to the risk involved. A good rule of thumb is to only take on risks where the potential reward significantly outweighs the potential loss. However, this ratio can vary depending on your business's stage and your personal risk tolerance.

Lastly, it's crucial to have a contingency plan. Things may not always go as expected, and having a fallback plan can help mitigate potential losses. This doesn't mean shying away from risky decisions but being prepared for different outcomes.

Remember, risk management is not about eliminating risk altogether but about making calculated decisions where the potential reward justifies the risk taken.

Learning from Bad Decisions

Every entrepreneur makes mistakes; it's an inevitable part of the journey. What distinguishes a great leader, however, is their ability to learn from these mistakes and turn them into stepping stones for future success.

Start by adopting a mindset that views failures as opportunities to learn. When a decision leads to an undesired outcome, step back and analyse what went wrong. Was it due to flawed decision-making process, external factors, or simply a bad judgment call? Being honest and critical with yourself is key.

Next, document these insights. Keep a decision journal where you record the reasoning behind each decision, the outcome and the lessons learned. This not only helps in avoiding similar mistakes in the future but also aids in honing your decision-making skills.

Moreover, share these lessons with your team. This not only fosters a culture of transparency and continuous improvement but also empowers your team to make better decisions themselves.

In conclusion, learning from bad decisions requires a proactive approach. By understanding what went wrong, adapting your decision-making process, and sharing the lessons learned, you turn temporary setbacks into valuable learning opportunities.

In mastering decision-making as a leader, you equip yourself with the tools to steer your business through the complexities of entrepreneurship. Whether it's choosing the right framework, balancing the scales of risk and reward, or learning from the missteps, each aspect of decision-making is a step towards becoming a more effective and inspiring leader. Remember, in the realm of leadership, every decision counts.

Time Management for Leaders

Prioritisation Techniques

In the dizzying daily grind of running a business, feeling like a circus juggler isn't uncommon. You've got balls in the air – sales, marketing, operations, you name it. But here's the kicker: not all balls are created equal. Some are made of glass, and some are rubber; drop a rubber one, and it bounces back. Drop a glass ball, and it shatters. So, how do you decide which balls to keep airborne? This is where effective prioritisation comes into play.

The Eisenhower Box, a simple yet profound tool, can revolutionise the way you prioritise tasks. It helps you sort tasks into four categories: urgent and important, important but not urgent, urgent but not important, and neither urgent nor important. The beauty is in its simplicity – tasks that are urgent and important must be done today. Those important but not urgent are scheduled. Tasks that are urgent but not important can be delegated (more on delegation later). Finally, eliminate those tasks that fit into neither category.

Another prioritisation strategy is the 80/20 rule, or Pareto Principle, which posits that 80% of results come from 20% of efforts. Identifying these 20% high-impact tasks can exponentially improve your productivity and effectiveness. This involves regularly analysing your business processes and outcomes to recalibrate your efforts towards those high-yield tasks.

Delegation Strategies

Delegation is not merely about offloading work; it's an art and a testament to effective leadership. It's about recognising that you aren't the superhero of every story told in your company – sometimes, you need a sidekick (or a few). The key to delegation lies in knowing what to delegate and to whom.

First, identify tasks that are low on your priority list but could be valuable learning opportunities for your team members. These are tasks where the risk of mistakes is manageable and where correction and feedback can lead to growth and improvement.

When delegating, clarity is your ally. Be clear about what the task is, why it's being done, and the expected outcomes. Set clear deadlines and standards for performance. It's also crucial to match tasks with employees' skills and career aspirations. This not only ensures that tasks are completed efficiently but also aids in the professional development of your team, keeping them motivated and engaged.

Remember, delegation is not abdication. Maintain a balance where you are not micromanaging but are still available to provide guidance and support. Regular check-ins and constructive feedback are vital components of successful delegation.

Tools for Managing Time Effectively

In today's digital age, a plethora of tools can aid in effective time management. Leveraging these can help you streamline processes, automate mundane tasks, and significantly free up your calendar to focus on high-value activities.

Project management tools like Asana or Trello can help you visualise project timelines, track progress, and manage tasks across teams. These tools facilitate better communication and collaboration, ensuring everyone is on the same page and reducing the time spent on meetings and follow-ups.

For those pesky tasks that eat into your productive time, tools like Zapier or IFTTT can be lifesavers. These automation tools help you create workflows that automatically handle repetitive tasks such as data entry, scheduling social media posts, or even sending out routine emails.

Lastly, cannot emphasise enough the importance of a good old-fashioned calendar. Whether it's Google Calendar or Outlook, mastering your calendar is a cornerstone of effective time management. Time blocking is a particularly useful technique where you divide your day into blocks of time, each dedicated to a specific task or set of tasks. This not only helps in maintaining focus but also ensures that you're making progress in various areas of your business daily.

Time management is less about squeezing as many tasks into your day as possible and more about simplifying how you work, getting more done in less time, and freeing up resources to enjoy life outside of work. As a visionary entrepreneur, managing your time effectively allows you to excel in your business while also enjoying the journey. Embrace these strategies, tools, and mindsets, and watch as you transform not only your business but also your life.

RECAP AND ACTION ITEMS

Congratulations on navigating through the essential aspects of building your leadership foundation. By now, you've unpacked the significance of core values, the intricacies of decision-making, and the art of time management. Let's ensure these aren't just concepts, but tools you actively use to transform and lead.

1. Revisit and Refine Your Core Values: Take a moment this week to write down your core values. Are they clear and do they truly represent what you stand for? Discuss them with your team or a mentor to see if they resonate universally within your enterprise. This practice will not only solidify your own understanding but will also embed these values deeply into your company culture.

2. Apply Decision-Making Frameworks: Start by identifying a recent decision you made. Break it down using the frameworks discussed: What were the risks? What was the reward? Reflect on the outcome. Moving forward, use these frameworks as a checklist for your decisions, big or small. Remember, consistency is key in honing your decision-making skills.

3. Experiment with Time Management Tools: This coming week, pick one new time management tool or technique. It could be as simple as prioritising your day's tasks each morning or delegating more effectively. Track the impact it has on your productivity and stress levels. Adjust and experiment until you find what best suits your style of leadership.

4. Leading by Example: Integrate the principles you follow into your daily actions. Your team will learn more from what you do than what you say. Show them how decisions are made, values are upheld, and time is managed. This transparency not only builds trust but also empowers your team to mirror these practices.

Lastly, remember that leadership is a journey, not a destination. Each day offers a new opportunity to learn, to inspire, and to better yourself. Embrace these opportunities, and you'll continue to grow both your business and your character as a leader. Keep pushing the limits, and remember, the most exemplary leaders are those who empower others to succeed.

INSPIRING AND MOTIVATING TEAMS

"Leadership is not about being in charge. It is about taking care of those in your charge." – Simon Sinek

Mastering Communication

In the realm of business, particularly for entrepreneurs like yourself, mastering communication isn't just about talking more or sending out more emails. It's about ensuring that every word and every interaction counts. This part of the book delves into the core strategies, skills, and nuances of communication that can transform uncertain murmurs into clear, confident messages.

Effective Communication Strategies

To kick things off, let's talk about the backbone of successful entrepreneurial ventures: effective communication strategies. This isn't about mastering the art of small talk or sending newsletters on time—this is about crafting messages that resonate, influence, and drive action.

The first step is clarity. Be clear about what you want to convey. This sounds straightforward, but in the heat of business operations, your message can easily become muddled. Simplify your message. Ask yourself, "What is the one thing I want my team to understand?" This will help you avoid the common pitfall of over-communication, where you bombard your team with so much information that the main point gets lost.

Once your message is clear, consider your delivery. Timing is crucial. Choose the right moment to communicate important messages. For example, sharing a critical strategic pivot at the end of a long meeting when everyone is exhausted might not yield the attention it deserves. Instead, set a specific meeting with a clear agenda to ensure that all ears are tuned in.

Then there's the medium. In today's digital age, you have emails, Slack, Zoom, and a myriad other tools at your disposal. However, the medium must suit the message. While emails are great for detailed instructions or updates, they can be impersonal. Sometimes a face-to-face meeting or a video call can make a significant impact, particularly when you are discussing something that affects the direction or the morale of the team.

Lastly, feedback loops are essential. Communication is not a one-way street. Encourage feedback, and make it easy and non-threatening for your team to provide it. This not only helps you gauge the effectiveness of your communication but also fosters a culture of openness.

Active Listening Skills

Moving onto active listening, a skill often overshadowed by the more glamorous speaking part, yet equally, if not more, important. Active listening involves fully concentrating on what is being said rather than just passively hearing the message of the speaker.

Start by giving your full attention. This might mean setting aside your digital devices during conversations or closing your laptop during meetings. Show that you are listening through non-verbal cues such as nodding or maintaining eye contact. These gestures might seem small, but they go a long way in making the speaker feel valued.

Clarification is another key aspect of active listening. If there is something you do not understand, do not hesitate to ask for clarification. This not only ensures you fully comprehend the message but also signals to your speaker that their message is important to you.

Reflecting and summarizing what you have heard are practices that not only aid in your understanding but also in affirming that of your speaker's. Try to paraphrase what's been said back to the speaker. For example, "So, what you're saying is..." This technique helps in clearing any misconceptions right at the moment and strengthens the communication channel.

Communicating in Crises

Finally, let's address the elephant in the room - communicating in crises. When the waters are rough, your team looks to you, the captain of the ship, to guide them. How you communicate in these moments can make or break your team's spirit and resolve.

Firstly, be prompt in your communication. In a crisis, the longer you wait to communicate, the more room you leave for rumours and fear to proliferate. Address the issue head-on, and do it quickly.

Transparency is crucial. Shielding your team from bad news might seem like a protective gesture, but it often backfires. Be open about the situation's realities but also share your plan to navigate these challenges. This not only prepares your team for possible setbacks but also pulls them into the journey of overcoming them together.

Lastly, maintain a steady flow of updates. A crisis doesn't resolve at the flick of a switch. Regular updates about what's happening, what's being done, and what to expect can provide your team with a sense of stability and continued trust in your leadership.

By mastering these communication facets, you not only enhance your leadership but also empower your team to perform at their best. Effective communication fosters a healthy work environment that can weather the storms of entrepreneurship and sail smoothly towards success.

Motivation Techniques

Understanding intrinsic vs extrinsic motivation is the first port of call when you're shaping the drive within your team. Let's kick off with a crash course. Intrinsic motivation comes from within an individual, driven by personal satisfaction or passion for the work itself. Extrinsic motivation, on the other hand, is fuelled by external factors – think bonuses, promotions, public recognition. Both types play crucial roles, but their effectiveness can vary dramatically depending on the individual and the context.

To leverage these effectively, you first need to understand that not all your team members are wired the same way. Some might leap at the chance for a bonus, while others thrive on personal growth and achievement. The trick is in not applying a one-size-fits-all approach. Instead, observe and interact with your team to grasp what makes each person tick.

Now, moving on to what can really change the game: personalised motivation strategies. This is where you, as a leader, need to wear your Sherlock Holmes hat and do a bit of detective work. Start with one-on-one meetings; these are gold mines for insights into what motivates your team members. Ask them direct questions about what they enjoy in their work, what they dread, and what they aspire to achieve. This isn't just about being nosy — it's about gathering the intel you need to craft bespoke motivational strategies that ignite a genuine drive.

For instance, let's say you have a team member who loves learning new things. You might motivate this person by providing opportunities for training or taking on new projects that stretch their skills. Another might be motivated by leadership opportunities or even public recognition. Here, you could let them lead a session in a team meeting or give them a shout-out in a company-wide newsletter.

But how do you ensure these personalised motivators lead to real, tangible outcomes? This brings us to setting motivational goals. It's all well and good to understand what motivates your team and even to personalise your approach, but if you're not setting clear, achievable goals, all that effort is as good as wasted.

Goal setting is an art. Set the bar too high, and you risk demotivating your team due to the sheer unattainability. Set it too low, and you fail to challenge them, which can lead to boredom or complacency. The key is in setting SMART goals – Specific, Measurable, Achievable, Relevant, and Time-bound. But here's the kicker: involve your team in the goal-setting process. This not only ensures that the goals are realistic, but it also boosts their commitment to achieving them.

Let's play this out with an example. Imagine your team is lagging behind in sales. Instead of imposing a goal of increasing sales by 50% within a quarter, which might seem daunting, involve your team in a discussion. Find out what they think is achievable. Maybe they settle on a 30% increase but suggest additional support in certain areas like customer service or marketing. Now, not only do you have a more achievable goal, but you've also got a team that's more committed because they had a say in setting it.

While you're steering the ship towards these motivational strategies, don't forget to sprinkle in a bit of fun. Yes, fun! It's too easy to get caught up in targets and metrics, but remember, at the end of the day, a motivated team is one that enjoys what they do. Whether it's a quick game of ping-pong in the break room or an off-site day out, never underestimate the power of having fun. It can do wonders for motivation and can often be the simplest yet most effective strategy in your arsenal.

In conclusion, motivating a team is less about pushing people to work harder and more about pulling together a blend of strategies that recognise individual drivers while aligning them with the team's goals. By mastering this blend, you not only inspire your team but also transform the very dynamics of how work gets done in your organisation. So go ahead, experiment with these techniques and watch your team's motivation soar to new heights.

Building Team Cohesion

Fostering a collaborative environment, managing team dynamics, and celebrating team successes are not just items on a checklist. They are essential practices that can transform your team from a group of individuals working next to each other into a unified force capable of achieving remarkable things.

Fostering a Collaborative Environment

Creating a space where collaboration isn't just encouraged but is a natural way of operating is crucial for any entrepreneur aiming for success. Begin by setting the stage for open communication. This means establishing a platform where ideas can be shared freely without judgment. Encourage your team to speak up, share their thoughts, and contribute their ideas. This can be facilitated through regular brainstorming sessions where every idea is valued.

Technology plays a vital role here. Utilise tools that enhance collaborative efforts, such as project management software, real-time document editing, and communication platforms that allow for seamless interaction regardless of physical locations. It's about making sure everyone is on the same page and can contribute equally to a project.

Physical spaces matter too. If your team works on-site, design your workspace to encourage random interactions and spontaneous discussions. Open-plan offices, communal areas, and breakout rooms can change the way your team interacts and collaborates.

But fostering a collaborative environment goes beyond logistics and into the realm of culture. This means embedding collaboration into the core values of your organisation. Recognise and reward teamwork. When employees see that collaborative efforts are appreciated, they are more likely to embrace and promote this culture themselves.

Managing Team Dynamics

Understanding and managing team dynamics is pivotal. Dynamics can make or break the team's spirit and productivity. Start by getting to know your team members individually. Understand their strengths, weaknesses, work styles, and motivations. This knowledge will allow you to assemble a team in which members complement each other rather than clash.

Conflict is inevitable, but it doesn't have to be destructive. Establish clear conflict resolution protocols that focus on the issue and not the person. Encourage a culture where feedback is constructive and aimed at solutions, not blame. Training your team in conflict resolution and communication skills can turn potentially divisive situations into opportunities for growth and innovation.

Keep an eye on groupthink — a phenomenon where the desire for harmony in a group results in an irrational or dysfunctional decision-making outcome. Encourage diversity of thought by assigning devil's advocates in meetings or by holding 'no-holds-barred' sessions where challenging the status quo is expected.

Another aspect is to be aware of the informal leaders within your team. These are individuals who, regardless of their official title, influence and motivate others. Leveraging these natural leaders can help in driving the team forward and ensuring that the group acts cohesively.

Celebrating Team Successes

Finally, the glue that holds all these efforts together is recognising and celebrating team successes. This not only boosts morale but also reinforces the behaviours you want to see in your team. Make it a point to celebrate not just the big wins but also the small victories along the way. Whether it's completing a challenging project under tight deadlines or a team member going above and beyond their duties, acknowledging these efforts makes team members feel valued and appreciated.

Celebrations can be as simple or as elaborate as you deem appropriate. From a simple shout-out in a team meeting to an off-site team-building retreat, what matters is the act of recognition itself. It's also important to personalise how you celebrate these successes. Some team members might appreciate public recognition, while others might prefer a private thank-you note. Understanding what makes your team tick will make these celebrations more meaningful.

Another powerful way to celebrate team success is by sharing success stories both within and outside the company. Internally, this builds a narrative of success and sets a benchmark for what is achievable. Externally, it boosts your company's brand and can attract top talent who are excited to work in a thriving, collaborative environment.

By fostering a collaborative environment, managing team dynamics effectively, and celebrating team successes enthusiastically, you're not just running a business; you're leading a powerhouse. Remember, the strength of the wolf is the pack, and in business, fostering cohesion within your team is one of the most powerful strategies for sustainable success.

RECAP AND ACTION ITEMS

Congratulations on completing this pivotal chapter on Inspiring and Motivating Teams. You've now equipped yourself with tools that can transform the way you lead and energise your team. Remember, the art of mastering communication, from refining your active listening skills to navigating through crises, sets the foundation for any strong leader. The ability to communicate effectively is not just about speaking well but understanding and being understood.

Moving on to motivation, you've explored the nuances between intrinsic and extrinsic motivators and how these can be harnessed to propel your team members towards their peak performance. Tailoring your approach to fit individual needs and setting clear, motivational goals is not just beneficial; it's essential for cultivating an environment where each team member thrives

Lastly, fostering team cohesion ensures that the collective operates as more than the sum of its parts. Encouraging collaboration, managing team dynamics adeptly, and celebrating successes together are all practices that contribute to a robust, unified team.

Now, let's put these insights into action. Start by implementing one new communication strategy in your next team meeting. It could be as simple as allowing more time for questions, or introducing a 'listening moment' to ensure everyone's voices are heard.

Next, identify the key motivators for each of your team members. Arrange one-on-one sessions to discuss their personal and professional goals, and see how these align with the team's objectives. This understanding will allow you to personalise your motivational strategies effectively.

Finally, plan a team-building activity that is not just fun but also involves collaborative problem-solving. Observe how your team interacts and take notes. Post-activity, gather everyone to celebrate the wins and discuss what could be improved. This reflection will enhance your team's cohesion and readiness to tackle future challenges.

By taking these steps, you will not only inspire and motivate your team but also transform how you lead. Here's to leading beyond limits and achieving remarkable success together!

STRATEGIC LEADERSHIP

"Strategy is about making choices, trade-offs; it's about deliberately choosing to be different." — Michael Porter

Strategic Thinking

Understanding Strategic Thinking

Alright, let's dive straight into the deep end. Strategic thinking isn't just a fancy buzzword tossed around in boardrooms; it's the backbone of all great enterprises. It's what separates the leaders from the followers, the successful from the stagnant. As an entrepreneur, you're not just running a business; you're leading a venture through uncharted territories, and strategic thinking is your compass.

But what exactly is strategic thinking? It's a method of viewing problems and solutions with a broad perspective, considering the long-term impacts while being agile enough to handle the immediate demands of the business. It's about being insightful, not just about the market today but forecasting where it's headed tomorrow. This means thinking ahead, planning with foresight and ensuring that every action aligns with your larger mission.

Imagine playing chess. Strategic thinking is about knowing not just the next move, but several moves ahead. It's about understanding the synergy between different pieces and how they collectively contribute to a winning strategy. In your business, these pieces are your resources, your team, and your competitive environment, all of which need to be aligned and moving towards a unified goal.

Tools for Strategic Analysis

Now, knowing that you need to think strategically is one thing; knowing how to do it is another. This is where tools for strategic analysis come into play. These tools aren't just for the analysts or consultants; they are crucial for you, the entrepreneur, to make informed decisions that shape the future of your business.

1. **SWOT Analysis:** Start simple. SWOT stands for Strengths, Weaknesses, Opportunities, and Threats. This framework helps you look internally at your strengths and weaknesses, and externally at the opportunities available and threats facing your business. It's a snapshot of your current strategic position within the market.

2. **PESTLE Analysis:** This tool extends your radar to the macro environment. PESTLE stands for Political, Economic, Social, Technological, Legal, and Environmental factors. Understanding these external factors can help you anticipate market trends and position your business to ride the wave, rather than be crushed by it.

3. **Porter's Five Forces:** Developed by Michael E. Porter, this tool is fantastic for analysing your industry's competitive structure. It looks at five key forces that affect your industry: competitive rivalry, bargaining power of suppliers, bargaining power of buyers, threat of new entrants, and threat of substitute products or services. Knowing these forces helps you carve out a niche and defend against competitive threats.

4. **Scenario Planning:** This might sound a bit sci-fi, but it's incredibly practical. Scenario planning involves imagining different future scenarios based on varying factors like economic conditions, technological advances, or consumer trends. It's like creating a "what if?" map for your business. This doesn't just prepare you for possible futures; it sparks innovative ideas and proactive strategies.

Implementing Strategic Actions

Having the tools is one thing, but applying them is where the magic happens. Implementation is all about turning insight into action. It's great to have a vision, but without action, it's just a daydream. Here's how you can execute strategic actions effectively:

1. **Align Your Team:** Ensure that everyone in your team understands the big picture and their role in it. This alignment is crucial for cohesive action and to prevent drifts in focus.

2. **Set SMART Goals:** That's Specific, Measurable, Achievable, Relevant, and Time-bound goals. These criteria transform nebulous ideas into clear targets. They also make it easier to track progress and keep your team accountable.

3. **Create Feedback Loops:** Strategy isn't set in stone; it's dynamic. Establish mechanisms to regularly check the pulse of your strategy against the reality of its execution. Use both qualitative insights from team feedback and quantitative data from business metrics.

4. **Stay Agile:** Flexibility is key in a world where business conditions can shift rapidly. Be willing to adapt your strategy based on what works and what doesn't. This doesn't mean changing course at every minor obstacle but being responsive to substantial changes in the environment.

5. **Celebrate Wins and Learn from Losses:** Every result is a learning

opportunity. Celebrate the wins to motivate your team, but also dissect what didn't work. This continuous learning culture is what keeps your strategy vibrant and relevant.

Remember, strategic thinking is not a one-off exercise; it's an ongoing practice. It requires patience, persistence, and a willingness to learn continuously. As you master strategic thinking, you'll find that it not only guides your business decisions but also sharpens your leadership, helping you lead your venture not just effectively but exceptionally. Keep pushing the boundaries, keep thinking strategically, and watch as your business transforms from surviving to thriving.

Innovation in Leadership

In the realm of entrepreneurship, innovation isn't just a buzzword; it's the lifeblood that keeps your venture not only alive but thriving. Embracing innovation within the leadership framework doesn't just set you apart from competitors; it propels you into a position of influence and success. Here's how you can infuse innovation into your leadership style and cultivate an environment where creativity and groundbreaking ideas flourish.

Creating a culture of innovation

The foundation of a truly innovative company is its culture. But what does it mean to create a culture of innovation? It starts with fostering an environment where every team member feels empowered to voice novel ideas, take calculated risks, and pursue uncharted paths.

Firstly, think about the physical workspace. It might seem trivial, but the layout of your office can significantly impact how your team interacts and collaborates. Open spaces encourage open communication and the exchange of ideas. Consider incorporating areas specifically designed for brainstorming and casual meetings. Google's offices, with their open workspaces and recreational areas, are a prime example of this approach in action.

However, creating a culture of innovation goes beyond the physical environment; it requires a shift in mindset and attitudes. As a leader, your role is to model the behaviour you want to see. Show enthusiasm for new ideas and be the first to question the status quo. Encourage your team to experiment and accept that failure is often part of the process. Remember, if you're not occasionally failing, you might not be pushing the boundaries far enough.

Finally, think about recognition. Everyone likes to feel appreciated, and innovators are no exception. Set up a system to celebrate innovative ideas and their implementations, regardless of the outcome. This could be as simple as a monthly shout-out in a team meeting or as formal as an annual innovation award. Recognition not only boosts morale but also reinforces the kind of thinking you want to cultivate in your team.

Overcoming barriers to innovation

While the drive for innovation is commendable, numerous barriers can stifle your team's creative potential. Identifying and overcoming these obstacles is crucial for maintaining an innovative momentum.

One major barrier is the fear of failure. In many organisations, mistakes are seen as setbacks or grounds for punishment, which can stifle creativity and risk-taking. Combat this by reframing failures as learning opportunities and integrate this perspective into your leadership style. When a project doesn't go as planned, instead of focusing on the negatives, analyse what went wrong, what you could do differently next time, and how the experience has provided valuable insights.

Another common hurdle is resistance to change. Change can be unsettling, and even the most seasoned professionals might shirk when faced with drastic transformations. Tackle this by keeping communication lines open. Explain not just what is changing and how, but importantly, why. Help your team see the bigger picture and how their cooperation is vital for success.

Resource constraints can also curb your innovation efforts. Whether it's time, money, or talent, limitations are inevitable. However, constraints can often be the mother of invention. Encourage your team to think outside the box and come up with resourceful solutions. Remember, innovation isn't necessarily about having the best resources but about utilising your available resources in the best possible way.

Leading disruptive change

Leading disruptive change is perhaps the ultimate test of an innovative leader. Disruption isn't just about making incremental improvements but about revolutionising parts of your business to create a significant impact.

Start by ensuring you have a clear vision of what you want to achieve and why. This vision will be your anchor throughout the process and should be communicated clearly and compellingly to your entire organisation.

Next, assemble a dedicated team to drive this change. Look for individuals who are not only skilled but also adaptable, with a natural inclination towards innovation and problem-solving. These will be your change champions within the organisation.

As you implement disruptive changes, keep your focus on agility. The business landscape today is incredibly volatile, and flexibility can offer a significant advantage. Encourage rapid prototyping of ideas, and use feedback loops to make continuous improvements. This approach not only speeds up the innovation process but also helps mitigate risks associated with big changes.

Throughout the journey, keep your team motivated. Disruptive change can be demanding and stressful, and it's easy for morale to wane. Maintain open communication about the challenges and successes, and celebrate milestones, no matter how small.

In conclusion, weaving innovation into the fabric of your leadership style requires deliberate effort and strategic thinking. By fostering a culture of innovation, addressing barriers head-on, and leading disruptive change with determination and vision, you can ensure that your organisation not only survives but thrives in the ever-evolving business landscape. Embrace these practices, and watch as your team, your products, and your company transform and lead beyond limits.

Navigating Change

Planning for Change

As an entrepreneur, envisioning the future of your business is crucial, but planning how to navigate the waters of change is just as vital. Change, as you know, isn't just an occasional disturbance in the calm of your business operations; it's a constant and dynamic force that can dictate your company's trajectory.

First, acknowledge that change is inevitable and can come from any direction. It might be technological advancements, shifts in consumer behaviour, regulatory updates, or even global economic shifts. The key is not merely to react to change but to anticipate and prepare for it.

Start with a robust strategy that includes a clear vision of the future. What do you want your business to achieve? How will the industry likely evolve, and how can you position your company to lead rather than follow? This vision will guide your planning.

Next, develop multiple scenarios. Consider the best, worst, and most likely scenarios you might face in the next year, three years, or even a decade.

For each scenario, consider different responses. What resources will be required? What might be the potential risks and benefits of each approach? This isn't about predicting the future accurately but being prepared for various possibilities.

Keep your plans flexible. A rigid plan can be as dangerous as no plan at all. Build adaptability into your strategies to allow for rapid pivoting or subtle shifts as needed. This might mean diversifying your supplier base to avoid being caught in supply chain disruptions or investing in cross-training employees to fill multiple roles during personnel changes.

Lastly, don't forget to embed regular reviews in your schedule. As external conditions change, revisit and revise your plans accordingly. This iterative process ensures that your strategies remain relevant and responsive to the changing business landscape.

Leading through Uncertainty

Leading through uncertainty is perhaps one of the most daunting aspects of entrepreneurship. Uncertainty can paralyse decision-making, reduce morale and create chaos if not managed effectively. As a leader, your role is to act as the compass and anchor in these turbulent times.

Start by embracing uncertainty yourself. If you're visibly nervous or unsure, this will likely ripple through your company. Maintain a composed demeanour and demonstrate confidence in your team's abilities to handle challenges. This doesn't mean you should have all the answers; sometimes, being honest about the uncertainties while reinforcing a positive outlook can significantly reassure your team.

Communication is your strongest tool here. Keep lines of communication open and transparent. Share what you know, what you don't know, and how you plan to move forward. This clarity will prevent misinformation and rumours from undermining your team's morale and productivity.

Encourage a culture of resilience. Promote flexibility in processes and thinking among your team members. Encourage them to come up with creative solutions and consider unconventional ideas that could help navigate uncertain times. Recognise and reward these behaviours to reinforce their importance.

Also, focus on building and maintaining trust. In uncertain times, trust becomes even more crucial as a foundational element of team cohesion and morale. Ensure your actions consistently reflect your words and make decisions based on the company's core values and long-term vision.

Lastly, manage your own stress and encourage your team to manage theirs. Uncertainty can be mentally and emotionally taxing. Supporting mental health in the workplace, providing resources, and ensuring that employees feel supported personally and professionally can help maintain focus and performance even during the most challenging periods.

Communicating Changes Effectively

Effectively communicating changes is critical to successful navigation through new waters. Whether it's a shift in company strategy, a restructuring, or a new product line, how you communicate these changes can significantly impact how they are received and implemented.

Firstly, consider your messaging. What are the key points that need to be communicated? Why is this change happening, and what benefits does it bring to the company and to your team? Be clear and concise in your messaging to avoid ambiguity, which can often lead to resistance.

Timing and method of communication are also crucial. Provide information as soon as possible but choose a suitable medium. Major changes might warrant an all-hands meeting or a personalised email detailing the changes. For ongoing projects, regular updates could be communicated via newsletters or team meetings.

Remember, communication is a two-way street. Encourage feedback and be ready to listen to concerns or suggestions from your team. This not only helps in spotting potential issues early but also makes your team feel valued and involved in the process.

In communicating changes, also be mindful of the cultural context of your organisation. Tailor your communication strategies to fit the cultural norms and values of your team. This sensitivity can enhance acceptance and minimise friction.

In essence, navigating change isn't just about steering through rough waters but doing so in a way that keeps your team cohesive, engaged, and ready to meet whatever challenges come your way. Change is not just a phase but a journey, and like any journey, it requires preparation, leadership, and clear communication.

RECAP AND ACTION ITEMS

Congratulations on completing this deep dive into the core of Strategic Leadership. By now, you've equipped yourself with the essentials of strategic thinking, embraced the nuances of fostering innovation, and mastered the art of navigating through change. The journey from here involves putting these insights into practice, transforming your approach and, ultimately, your enterprise.

Let's begin by revisiting strategic thinking. You understand the importance of seeing the big picture and the mechanics of deploying strategic tools. Now, make it a regular practice to step back and analyse your business landscape. Set aside time each week to review your strategic position and update your objectives accordingly. This continuous loop of assessment and action will keep you on the path to long-term success.

Moving to innovation, you've seen how vital a culture of creativity is and recognised common hurdles. Your action here is to initiate regular brainstorming sessions that are open to all team members, regardless of their role. Encourage wild ideas, foster an environment where mistakes are seen as stepping stones, and keep a channel open for all voices to be heard. Remember, a single idea can pivot the entire business landscape.

Finally, in navigating change, you've grasped the importance of planning and the dynamics of leading through uncertainty. Start by developing a clear change management strategy. Define the roles and responsibilities, prepare contingency plans, and ensure there are ample resources to support the change process. Communication is your golden ticket here; ensure it is clear, consistent, and compassionate to guide your team through the transition smoothly.

By integrating these strategies into your daily leadership practice, you're not just running a business; you're spearheading a visionary enterprise. Keep the momentum going, stay curious, and lead with the courage to transform challenges into opportunities for growth. Here's to your continued success as a strategic leader!

Now, take these insights, make them your own, and lead your business beyond limits!

THE POWER OF INFLUENCE

"Influence is not manipulation - it is helping people think about things in a way they've never thought about them before." - Kim Scott

Understanding Influence

Influence, is quite the buzzword in the entrepreneurial sphere, isn't it? It's about steering the boat rather than rowing it, leading rather than following. As a business owner or entrepreneur, understanding the mechanics of influence can radically transform your approach to leadership and growth. So, let's break it down into three critical components: the psychology of influence, building credibility and trust, and differentiating influence from manipulation.

The Psychology of Influence

At its core, influence is about understanding and navigating human emotions and decision-making processes. It's psychological. You're not just selling a product or a service; you're offering feelings, experiences, and identities. Think about the last time you bought something – was it just because you needed it, or did it make you feel a certain way? That's the psychology of influence at play.

Robert Cialdini, a name synonymous with understanding this concept, outlines principles like reciprocity, commitment, social proof, authority, liking, and scarcity in his seminal work. Each principle taps into basic human instincts. For example, the principle of reciprocity suggests that people feel obliged to give back to others who have given to them. In business, this could be as simple as providing a free trial or a sample. It's not just about being nice;

it's strategic, fostering a sense of obligation in potential customers.

Next, think about commitment. If you can get a commitment from someone, they are more likely to act consistently with that commitment because of aligning with their self-image. Free trials again play into this. Once customers start using your product, they're more likely to continue using (and paying for) it, rather than switching to a competitor.

Understanding these psychological triggers allows you to craft strategies that don't just chase sales but build a narrative that your customers want to be part of.

Building Credibility and Trust

Trust is the bedrock of effective influence. Without trust, even the most sophisticated psychological strategies can fall flat. Building credibility and trust is less about what you say and more about what you do.

First, consider transparency. Being open about your business practices, successes, and failures makes you relatable and trustworthy. It's like letting customers behind the curtain of a magic show they appreciate the honesty and are more likely to become loyal advocates for your brand.

Consistency is another key player. Consistency in your message, your values, and your delivery builds a reliable brand image. If customers know what to expect from you, they're more comfortable investing their time and money into what you're offering. This doesn't mean you can't evolve, but your core messages should be coherent and steady.

Lastly, expertise. You need to show that you know your stuff. This could be through thought leadership, such as publishing articles, giving talks, or maintaining an active and insightful presence on social media. When people see you as an authority in your field, they trust your advice and your products.

Influence vs Manipulation

This is a crucial distinction. While influence focuses on mutual benefit, manipulation exploits for personal gain. Ethical influence respects and values the agency of others, offering choices and enhancing relationships. Manipulation, on the other hand, often involves deceit and coercion, leading to short-term gains but long-term losses, particularly in terms of reputation and trust.

Understanding this difference is vital. When you influence ethically, you build long-term relationships that support sustainable business growth. Your audience should feel empowered and better off for having interacted with you—not cheated or coerced.

For example, let's say you're launching a new product. An influential approach might involve demonstrating how the product solves a problem or improves life, backed by honest testimonials and clear, fair pricing. A manipulative approach might involve exaggerated claims, hidden fees, or high-pressure sales tactics that leave customers feeling tricked once the truth comes out.

As an entrepreneur, your aim should be clear: to cultivate influence that respects and uplifts others, creating a network of support and enthusiasm around your ventures. This ethical approach not only fosters trust and credibility but also establishes you as a leader in your industry—a leader who not only aims to succeed but also to contribute positively to the community and market you serve.

With these insights into the psychology of influence, strategies for building credibility and trust, and a clear understanding of the fine line between influence and manipulation, you're well-equipped to lead with integrity and impact. Remember, influence is not just about reaching the top; it's about lifting others along your journey. Embrace these principles, and watch not just your business, but also your relationships flourish.

Networking and Relationships

Building strong business networks is akin to constructing a resilient bridge that connects you to a myriad of opportunities. As an entrepreneur, the quality of your networks often determines the altitude of your career trajectory. It's not merely about collecting business cards or adding contacts on LinkedIn; it's about forging relationships that are both meaningful and beneficial. The art of networking isn't something that's innate; it s cultivated through strategy, sincerity, and a bit of savvy.

Firstly, understand that your network should be diverse. This diversity should span various industries, professions, and roles. It's easy to stay within the comfort zone of your industry, but the magic happens when you step outside this bubble. Cross-industry connections can inspire innovative ideas and offer new perspectives that you won't find in an echo chamber of similar professionals.

Active involvement in both local and global professional groups can also significantly bolster your network. Whether it's a local chamber of commerce or an international trade association, each of these groups provides a platform to meet individuals who can offer insights and opportunities that can propel your business forward. Remember, the key is active participation. Attend meetings, volunteer for committees, and speak at events. Visibility is credibility in these circles.

Another potent strategy is to leverage technology to network. Virtual forums, webinars, and online workshops provide opportunities to connect with global talents and thought leaders. These platforms are not limited by geographical boundaries and can be particularly beneficial if your business has a global scope.

Moving on to leveraging relationships for mutual benefit, it's essential to approach networking with a mindset of giving rather than taking. Before asking for favours, think about how you can provide value to others. Perhaps you can offer your expertise, make an introduction, or provide a resource that could benefit someone else in your network. This approach not only enriches your relationships but also establishes your reputation as a generous and valuable member of your network.

Effective networking is not a one-time activity but a continuous process of nurturing relationships. Regular check-ins via emails, sharing relevant articles, or even informal coffee meetings can keep the relationship alive and top of mind. When the time comes that you need support or collaboration, these contacts are more likely to recall your previous generosity and respond in kind.

Furthermore, in every interaction, ensure clarity in communication about what you can offer and what you seek. Ambiguity can lead to misunderstandings and missed opportunities. Be specific about your skills and needs while remaining open to unexpected ways in which you might be able to collaborate.

For introverted leaders, networking might seem daunting, but it doesn't have to be. Introverts bring unique strengths to networking, such as a propensity for deep conversations and a natural inclination towards listening. These qualities can be powerful in forming deeper connections.

One effective strategy for introverted leaders is to focus on quality over quantity. Instead of trying to meet everyone in the room, aim for meaningful interactions with a few individuals. Prepare some questions or topics in advance to ease into conversations. Discussing subjects you are passionate about can help the dialogue flow more naturally and be more engaging.

Another tactic is to leverage your existing network to make new connections. Starting with mutual connections can make the context more comfortable and the introduction smoother. Also, consider smaller, more intimate networking settings, such as roundtable discussions or workshops, where interaction feels more manageable and less overwhelming.

Lastly, utilise social media and professional networking sites like LinkedIn to initiate connections before meeting in person. This approach can help to break the ice and make you feel more comfortable when you eventually meet face-to-face.

In conclusion, networking for business leaders isn't just about expanding your contact list. It's about strategically building and nurturing relationships that are mutually beneficial. By understanding the value of diverse, robust networks, offering value before seeking it, and adapting strategies to suit your personality, you can enhance your influence and drive your business towards greater success. Remember, the power of networking lies in the quality of relationships, not merely the quantity of contacts.

Persuasion Techniques

Principles of Persuasion

In the world of business, the ability to sway opinions and encourage action is not just beneficial; it's essential. One of the most respected frameworks for understanding this art is Robert Cialdini's six principles of persuasion, which are reciprocity, commitment and consistency, social proof, authority, liking, and scarcity.

Reciprocity is the simple law of give and take. People are wired to return favours. As an entrepreneur, providing value first—whether it's a free sample, a helpful insight, or a useful tool—can create a sense of obligation in others, which you can leverage when you make your requests.

Commitment and consistency are about people's desire to align with their past behaviour. If you can encourage a small initial commitment, the chances are higher that individuals will agree to more significant requests later. This is particularly effective in negotiations and sales, where an initial small agreement can lead to a larger sale.

Social proof, the third principle, capitalises on the human tendency to follow the actions of the masses. Showing that others like your client or customer have made similar decisions can significantly boost your influence. Testimonials, case studies, and widespread social media shares are practical tools here.

Authority involves proving your expertise and credibility. When people recognise that you have a profound knowledge or specialised skill set, they're more likely to be persuaded by what you say. Achieving this might mean public speaking, publishing articles, or gaining endorsements from other respected figures in your industry.

Liking — people are easily persuaded by individuals they like. Building rapport and showing genuine interest in your counterparts can substantially enhance your persuasive power. Remember, small talk isn't just a filler; it's a bridge to fostering stronger connections.

Lastly, scarcity. The principle that limited access increases desirability. Highlighting the exclusivity or the limited availability of your offer can act as a powerful motivator for decision-makers. It's not just about making a good offer but also about making it feel special.

Crafting Persuasive Messages

Crafting a message that persuades involves more than stringing together compelling words; it involves strategically structuring your communication to resonate deeply with your audience. Start with clarity—be clear about what you're offering and why it matters to your listener. Ambiguity can be the enemy of persuasion, as confusion often leads to inaction.

Next, focus on the benefits rather than the features. While the specifics of a product or service are important, what truly moves people is understanding how it improves their lives or business. For example, rather than highlighting the technical specifications of a software tool, you could emphasise how it will save time, reduce costs, or increase revenue.

The structure of your message also impacts its effectiveness. The classic problem-solution-benefit format is a proven strategy. Lead with a relatable problem or pain point, offer your proposition as the solving mechanism, and close by clearly outlining the benefits of taking the proposed action.

Emotional appeal is another critical component. Humans are not always rational beings; we are driven by emotions. Tapping into feelings like fear, excitement, or happiness can propel people towards action. However, ensure your emotional appeals are ethical and do not manipulate or deceive.

Finally, end with a strong call to action. Be specific about what you want your audience to do next—whether it's to sign up, call a number, or schedule a meeting. A compelling call to action turns your persuasive message into a pathway for engagement and action.

Persuasive Speaking for Leaders

As a leader, your ability to speak persuasively is pivotal. It can be the difference between inspiring your team and being met with indifference. Effective persuasive speaking starts with confidence. You need to believe in what you're saying if you expect others to do the same. This confidence shouldn't come from a place of arrogance but from genuine belief in your message.

Structure your speech effectively. Begin with a strong opening that grabs attention—this could be a startling statistic, a provocative question, or a compelling story. The body of your speech should reinforce your central message, using evidence, stories, and examples to build your case. Each point should flow logically to the next, leading seamlessly into a powerful conclusion that reinforces your primary message and includes a clear call to action.

Varying your tone and pace can also keep your audience engaged. Monotony is the death of persuasion. By varying your delivery, you create energy and emphasis, helping to ensure that your key points stick.

Remember also to engage with your audience. Make eye contact, ask rhetorical questions, or even invite direct questions depending on the setting. Engagement transforms your speech from a monologue into a dialogue, making it more persuasive.

Lastly, practise empathy. Understanding your audience's needs, fears, and desires allows you to tailor your message and delivery style in a way that resonates. This connection is crucial—it's not just about what you say, but also about making your audience feel understood and valued.

Through mastering these techniques, your ability to persuade as a leader will not only grow; it will flourish, allowing you to inspire action, drive change, and lead more effectively. Remember, persuasion is an art, but also a skill that can be honed with practice and persistence.

RECAP AND ACTION ITEMS

You've just navigated through the intricate maze of influence, unpacking its psychological underpinnings, the essence of trustworthiness, and the delicate balance between influence and manipulation. You've also explored the dynamics of networking and relationship-building, along with strategies tailored for even the most introverted leaders. Finally, you've been armed with persuasive techniques that can elevate your leadership communication to new heights.

Now, let's translate these insights into concrete steps that you can take to magnify your influence within your business and beyond.

1. **Assess Your Influence Style:** Start by reflecting on your current approach to influence. Are you more of a persuader or a collaborator? Do you rely on data or on emotional appeal? Understanding your natural style will help you identify areas for improvement and further development.

2. **Commit to Building Trust:** Trust is the foundation of effective influence. Make a plan to enhance your credibility among peers, employees, and partners. This could involve transparent communication, consistent actions, or sharing your successes and failures openly.

3. **Set Networking Goals:** Define clear, achievable goals for expanding your business network. Perhaps aim to connect with three new people in your industry each month or attend one significant networking event per quarter. Remember, quality often trumps quantity in relationships.

4. **Create a 'Mutual Benefit' Mindset:** Whenever you engage in networking, approach each interaction with the question, "How can we create value for each other?" This mindset will not only expand your network but deepen the relationships within it, creating opportunities for collaboration.

5. **Develop a Persuasion Toolkit:** Based on the principles of persuasion you've learned, develop a toolkit that includes key phrases, storytelling techniques, and the effective use of data. Tailor this toolkit to different scenarios, such as pitching to investors, selling to customers, or motivating your team.

6. **Practice Persuasive Speaking:** Whether it's through a local speaking club, workshops, or even virtual meetings, regularly put your persuasive speaking skills to test. The more you practice, the more natural and effective your public speaking will become.

7. **Reflect and Revise Regularly:** Influence is not static. Regularly reflect

on your interactions and experiences. What worked? What didn't? Adapt your strategies accordingly, staying responsive to changes in your business environment and feedback from your network.

By integrating these actions into your routine, you'll not only see a boost in your ability to influence others but also witness a transformation in your personal leadership style and business success. Remember, the power of influence lies in consistent, authentic, and strategic application. Start small, think big, and keep growing. Your journey to becoming a more influential leader in the business world continues from here.

DEVELOPING LEADERSHIP SKILLS

"Leadership and learning are indispensable to each other." - John F. Kennedy

Continuous Learning

In the fast-evolving landscape of business, the ability to keep learning is akin to keeping your boat steadily afloat in choppy waters. As a visionary entrepreneur, you're not just the captain of your ship but also its chief navigator, and continuous learning is your compass. Let's dive into how embracing lifelong learning, tapping into resources for leadership development, and learning from mentors can significantly enhance your leadership skills.

Embracing Lifelong Learning

The notion of lifelong learning isn't new, but its importance has skyrocketed in an era where business models, technology, and market dynamics shift at breakneck speed. Embracing lifelong learning is less about formal education and more about cultivating a mindset that thirsts for knowledge and understanding, regardless of your age or success level.

Imagine this: every piece of knowledge you acquire is a tool in your entrepreneurial toolkit. The more tools you have, the more versatile and adept you become at tackling different challenges and seizing opportunities. It's about staying relevant and capable in a world where relevance is your currency.

How do you cultivate this mindset? Start by setting personal learning goals related to both your personal and professional life. Whether it's learning a new language that might open up international market opportunities, or mastering the latest digital marketing strategies to boost your online presence, the key is to keep your learning objectives aligned with your business goals.

Moreover, make learning a habit. Dedicate time in your busy schedule, even if it's just an hour a week, to read, listen, or engage in a learning activity. It could be as simple as reading industry-specific articles, listening to podcasts by thought leaders, or attending webinars. The method isn't as important as the commitment to the process.

Resources for Leadership Development

In your journey as a leader, not all your learning will come from books or classrooms. Much of it will come from resources that you might not have considered part of your learning ecosystem. For leadership development, look beyond the conventional and consider these avenues:

1. **Online Platforms:** Websites like Coursera, Udemy, and LinkedIn Learning offer a plethora of courses designed specifically for leadership development. These platforms provide flexibility and a wide range of topics, from strategic decision-making to emotional intelligence in leadership.

2. **Professional Groups and Networks:** Joining groups like the Entrepreneurs' Organization (EO) or The Young Presidents' Organization (YPO) can be immensely beneficial. These groups not only offer a platform for professional growth but also provide exposure to new and diverse perspectives through peer interaction.

3. **Conferences and Workshops:** Regularly attending industry-specific or leadership-focused conferences can be a goldmine for learning current best practices and trends. Workshops provide a hands-on opportunity to refine new skills in a practical environment.

4. **Books and Publications:** Don't underestimate the power of a good book. Authors like Simon Sinek and Brené Brown offer invaluable insights into leadership that are both timeless and revolutionary. Subscribe to or regularly read business and leadership magazines and journals like Harvard Business Review or Forbes to stay updated on the latest in business thought leadership.

Learning from Mentors

The role of mentors in shaping leaders is immeasurable. Mentors are the secret sauce to many a successful entrepreneur's journey. They provide not just guidance but also an experienced sounding board for your ideas.

Finding the right mentor can sometimes feel like looking for a needle in a haystack, but knowing what you need is half the battle won. Identify what gaps you need to fill in your own experience or knowledge, and seek out individuals who best represent the skills or achievements you aspire to. Remember, mentoring doesn't always follow a formal structure. It can be as informal as periodic conversations with someone you admire within your network, or it could be a more structured relationship defined by regular meetings and goals.

Once you find a mentor, be proactive about the relationship. Come to each meeting prepared with questions or topics to discuss. Be open to feedback, even if it's not always what you want to hear. A good mentor doesn't just pat you on the back; they challenge you to grow and think differently.

Moreover, consider reverse mentoring – where you learn from someone younger or less experienced. This can be particularly valuable in areas like technology and emerging consumer trends, where younger generations often have their finger on the pulse.

In conclusion, the journey of learning never really stops, especially not for someone steering a business. By embracing lifelong learning, leveraging diverse resources for leadership development, and actively seeking and engaging with mentors, you equip yourself with the resilience, knowledge, and versatility needed to lead effectively and keep your business thriving in an ever-changing world. Remember, the more you learn, the more you realize how much there is to learn. Embrace this journey with enthusiasm and an open mind, and watch as every new piece of knowledge adds depth and value to your leadership style and business success.

Feedback and Critiques

When it comes to honing your leadership skills, mastering the art of both giving and receiving feedback is as crucial as it is challenging. As an entrepreneur, your ability to interact constructively with feedback can significantly influence your personal growth and the development of your business.

Giving and Receiving Feedback

Let's kick off with the basics: feedback is a two-way street. You're not just doling out advice and evaluations; you're also on the receiving end. How you handle both roles plays a pivotal part in shaping your leadership style.

Firstly, when giving feedback, it's essential to ensure it's constructive. The goal is to foster growth and improvement, not to demoralise. Start with something positive. This doesn't mean sugarcoating the issues, but rather acknowledging the strengths before addressing areas for improvement. It's about striking a balance. For instance, if an employee has faltered in a project, acknowledge their effort or a particular aspect they handled well, before moving on to what could have been done better.

As you deliver feedback, be specific. Vague comments can lead to confusion and frustration. Instead of saying, "You need to be more proactive," specify with examples, like, "I noticed in the last few meetings, you haven't shared many ideas. Maybe next time, you could come prepared with a couple of suggestions that we could discuss."

Now, flipping the script—receiving feedback. This can be tough, especially when it's not as positive as you'd hope. The key here is to listen actively. Resist the urge to defend yourself or explain. When you're on the receiving end, try to view feedback as a valuable data point, not a personal attack. After the feedback session, take some time to process the information. Reflect on it and plan how you can apply this to your growth. Remember, the most successful leaders are those who see feedback as an opportunity, not a setback.

Constructive Criticism

Moving deeper into the realm of feedback, constructive criticism is an art form in itself. It's about more than just pointing out what's wrong; it's about encouraging change and improvement. As a leader, mastering this can transform your communication and relationships within your team.

When delivering constructive criticism, context is everything. Ensure that the setting is appropriate—private feedback should never be given in public spaces. This respects the individual's feelings and helps maintain their confidence and dignity.

Use "I" statements to soften the blow. Instead of saying, "You didn't handle that client well," try, "I feel that the situation with the client could have been handled differently. Perhaps we could discuss some alternative approaches?" This shifts the focus from the person to the situation.

Timing is also critical. Offering feedback immediately after an incident can be effective as the details are fresh. However, in situations where emotions are high, it's wise to wait until things have cooled down. This delay allows for more rational and productive conversation.

Using Feedback for Personal Growth

Finally, the ultimate goal of feedback and critiques isn't just to inform but to transform. Feedback should be a tool that you use to propel yourself and your business forward.

Start by creating a feedback-friendly culture in your business. Encourage open channels of communication where feedback is regularly exchanged. Make it a norm, not an exception. This can be facilitated through regular review sessions, where both you and your team can share insights and constructive critiques.

Moreover, act on the feedback you receive. It's not enough to just collect feedback; you must also implement it. Identify the key takeaways from each feedback session and set concrete steps for improvement. Maybe it's a skill you need to develop, a course you should take, or a change in your approach to leadership.

Remember to track your progress. Set benchmarks and review them regularly. This not only keeps you accountable but also allows you to see how far you've come. It can be incredibly motivating to look back and realise that the feedback which once seemed daunting has now paved the way for substantial growth.

In conclusion, while feedback and critiques can sometimes be hard to swallow, they are indispensable tools for any entrepreneur serious about leadership. By learning to give effective feedback and embracing every critique as a learning opportunity, you're setting yourself—and your business—up for continued success and innovation. Embrace feedback with open arms and a willing mind, and watch as it transforms not just your business operations, but your entire approach to leadership.

Leadership Training Programmes

When you're on the hunt for the right leadership training programme, the sheer number of options can seem like you're a kid in a sweet shop, yet with the paradox of choice comes the risk of indecision. How do you sift through the glitter to find the gold? Let's dive into how to evaluate these courses, tailor them to your unique entrepreneurial needs, and most crucially, implement what you learn so it doesn't just remain theory.

Evaluating leadership courses

Kicking off with evaluating leadership courses, the process is akin to Sherlock Holmes meets your inner venture capitalist. You're not just spending money; you're investing in your future self. The first step? Look beyond the glossy brochures and charismatic sales pitches. Start with the curriculum. What skills are they teaching? Do they match what you're lacking or what your business needs next? You're looking for substance over style, real skills that can propel you and your business forward, not just nice-to-have credentials for your LinkedIn profile.

Next, check out who's behind the curtain. Who are the instructors? Look for programmes where leaders who have actually walked the walk – those who have been in the trenches and come out the other side with businesses and reputations intact – are teaching. Their experience is gold dust for anyone looking to climb the slippery ladder of success.

Moreover, don't skip on the peer reviews. What are previous participants saying? Look for reviews that speak about long-term impacts, not just immediate satisfaction. It's easy to feel high on inspiration right after a course, but the real test is whether attendees implement and benefit from the teachings weeks, months, or even years later.

Finally, consider the format and timing. Does it fit with your current commitments? As an entrepreneur, your time is precious. Ensure the course format - be it online, in-person, part-time, or intensive - aligns with your lifestyle and business demands. You want a programme that stretches you but doesn't snap you.

Tailoring training to your needs

Now, tailoring a training programme to your needs might feel like trying to fit a square peg into a round hole. It doesn't have to. Start with a clear understanding of your endgame. What specific leadership gaps are you trying to fill? Are you looking to boost your strategic thinking, or perhaps your team's morale could use a lift? Maybe it's the nitty-gritty of financial management that's currently your Achilles' heel?

Armed with this insight, approach your chosen programme with a mindset of personalisation. Speak to the coordinators. Can they tweak the content to better suit your objectives? Some programmes offer modular or elective components that can be more closely aligned with your goals. This approach not only maximises the relevance of your learning but also ensures that you're not sitting through sessions that are of little benefit.

Additionally, consider your learning style. Do you absorb more through interaction and practical challenges, or do you prefer lectures and notes? Ensure the course's teaching style aligns with how you learn best. This alignment significantly increases the likelihood that you'll not only retain information but also enjoy the process.

Implementing learning into practice

Finally, the rubber hits the road with implementation. All the knowledge in the world won't drive your business forward if it's left gathering dust in your brain's back shelves. Implementation begins with setting actionable goals during the course itself. What concrete steps will you take post-course?

Maybe it's a new morning briefing routine with your team or a revised risk management strategy.

Keep yourself accountable or even better, get someone else to hold you to account. This could be a mentor, a business partner, or a fellow course participant. Discuss your implementation goals with them, set specific check-ins, and get ready to report on your progress.

It's also about fostering a culture of learning within your company. Share your insights with your team. This not only reinforces what you've learned but also encourages a broader culture of personal development within your team. When everyone is learning and growing, the business accelerates.

Moreover, keep the loop of feedback spinning. As you implement new strategies or leadership styles, gather feedback. What's working? What isn't? This feedback is invaluable and can help you tweak your approach continuously.

In essence, choosing the right leadership training programme isn't just about upskilling yourself; it's about setting in motion a cycle of growth, feedback, and continuous improvement that propels not just you but your entire business forward. Remember, in the dynamic theatre of business, standing still is not an option. Keep moving, keep learning, and keep leading beyond limits.

RECAP AND ACTION ITEMS

Congratulations on navigating through the crucial aspects of developing your leadership skills. You now have the tools to engage in continuous learning, handle feedback effectively, and choose the right leadership training programmes that resonate with your unique entrepreneurial journey.

First off, let's solidify your commitment to lifelong learning. Set up a monthly routine where you explore new resources, be it books, podcasts, or webinars, focusing on leadership and growth. Dedicate at least one hour a week to this endeavour. Remember, the key here is consistency.

Next, create a feedback system in your daily operations. This could involve setting up regular review sessions with your team or having a feedback box where ideas can be anonymously submitted. Use the insights gathered to refine your approach, knowing that each piece of feedback is a golden nugget towards personal and professional excellence.

Now, let's talk action on the leadership training front. Research and identify at least two programmes or workshops that align with your current leadership challenges and future goals. Commit to attending these programmes within the next six months to ensure you're not just learning passively but actively enhancing your leadership toolbox.

Finally, implementation is crucial. After each learning session, whether it's a formal training or an insightful conversation with a mentor, take a moment to jot down key takeaways and actionable steps. Schedule a time each week to review these and integrate them into your business practices.

By taking these steps, you not only evolve as a leader but also drive your business towards greater heights. Remember, the path of leadership is continuous and ever-evolving. Embrace it, and watch as you transform challenges into opportunities for growth and innovation.

LEADING HIGH-PERFORMANCE TEAMS

> "Coming together is a beginning. Keeping together is progress. Working together is success." – Henry Ford

Team Performance Metrics

In the world of high-performance teams, understanding how to gauge success is crucial. As an entrepreneur, you're not just in charge of steering the ship but also need to keep a keen eye on how effectively your crew rows. Let's dive into the essentials of setting performance standards, monitoring team performance, and employing the right tools to measure success.

Setting Performance Standards

First things first, setting performance standards is akin to drawing a map for a treasure hunt. You define what treasure looks like so everyone knows exactly what they're digging for. It's about creating clear, achievable, and measurable goals that align with your business's overarching objectives. Remember, if the standards are too vague, you're setting the stage for confusion; too stringent, and you risk demotivating your team. It's all about balance.

Start by identifying key performance indicators (KPIs) that resonate with your business's goals. Are you driving towards revenue targets, looking to boost customer satisfaction, or aiming to cut down operational costs? Whatever your focus, your KPIs should be SMART: Specific, Measurable, Achievable, Relevant, and Time-bound. For instance, rather than saying "increase sales," a SMART KPI would be "increase sales by 15% in Q1."

Engage with your team when setting these standards. This isn't just about handing down goals from on high; it's about creating a collaborative environment where goals are shared and understood by everyone. This approach not only clarifies expectations but also fosters a sense of ownership and commitment among team members.

Monitoring Team Performance

With your standards set, the next step is monitoring. Think of yourself as a coach during a high-stakes game. You can't just set the play and hope for the best; you need to watch how things unfold and be ready to make real-time adjustments.

Regular check-ins are your best friend here. This doesn't mean micromanaging every aspect of your team's work, but rather setting up a system where progress can be assessed periodically. Whether it's weekly summaries, monthly meetings, or quarterly reviews, the key is consistency. These check-ins should be structured and focused on discussing the data behind the performance. It's not just about what is or isn't working, but why.

Utilising performance management software can streamline this process. These tools can provide real-time data and analytics, helping you spot trends, identify bottlenecks, and acknowledge successes. Moreover, they can enhance transparency within your team, as everyone can see their progress and understand how their efforts contribute to the company's goals.

Feedback plays a crucial role here. It should be a two-way street where team members feel comfortable discussing hurdles and successes. Constructive feedback helps in adjusting strategies promptly and reinforces the message that every team member's input is valued in shaping the journey towards achieving set goals.

Tools for Measuring Success

In today's digital age, the tools at your disposal for measuring success are vast and varied. Choosing the right ones can make a significant difference in how you understand and influence your team's performance.

Start with performance management tools. Platforms like Monday.com, Asana, or Trello can help manage tasks and monitor progress against specific objectives. These tools are incredibly useful in breaking down large goals into manageable tasks, making it easier for team members to stay on track and for you to monitor progress.

Analytics tools also play a critical role. Google Analytics, for example is indispensable for tracking online engagement and can be crucial for businesses whose operations have a significant digital component. For sales teams, CRM software like Salesforce provides detailed insights into customer interactions, sales pipelines, and more.

Don't overlook the power of employee engagement tools. Platforms like Officevibe or TinyPulse can give you a deeper insight into how engaged your team is, which is a critical component of overall performance. These tools can help you gauge the mood and morale of your team, offering anonymous feedback options that can encourage more honest and constructive responses.

Choosing the right tools will depend heavily on your specific business needs and the areas you've identified as critical for monitoring. The goal here is not just to collect data, but to turn that data into actionable insights that drive your team forward.

In leading high-performance teams, your role as an entrepreneur extends beyond just setting goals and expectations. It's about actively engaging with your team to set clear standards, monitor progress effectively, and utilise the right tools to measure and enhance performance. By mastering these elements, you're not just chasing success; you're setting up a structured path to achieve it, ensuring that everyone on your team knows where they're going and what's expected of them.

Conflict Resolution

Identifying Sources of Conflict

In the fast-paced world of entrepreneurship, conflict is as inevitable as the next big idea. The first step to mastering conflict resolution within your team is to pinpoint where these conflicts typically stem from. Understanding the root causes can help you anticipate potential problems and address them proactively.

One common source of conflict is miscommunication. This can happen when team members are not clear about their roles or the expectations set upon them. It might manifest as missed deadlines or overlapping duties, which can lead to frustration and resentment among team members. Another frequent culprit is differences in personality and work styles. What energises one person might be a pet peeve for another, and without a common ground, tension can escalate.

Resource allocation can also lead to disputes within a team. When team members feel they're competing for limited resources—whether it's time, money, or attention from leadership—conflict can naturally arise. Lastly, resistance to change is a significant source of conflict, especially in high-growth environments where adaptability is crucial. Some team members might struggle with or resist changes in processes, which can lead to internal conflicts.

By keeping an eye out for these common conflict catalysts, you can better prepare to address them before they fester into bigger issues.

Strategies for Conflict Resolution

Once you've identified potential sources of conflict, the next step is to resolve these issues in a way that not only diffuses tension but also strengthens your team. Here are some strategies you might find effective:

1. **Open Communication:** Encourage an environment where team members feel safe expressing their thoughts and feelings. When everyone is open about their concerns and listens actively, many conflicts can be resolved easily. Establish regular check-ins and feedback loops to facilitate this.

2. **Define Clear Roles and Responsibilities:** When everyone knows what is expected of them, there's less room for confusion and conflict. Make sure roles and responsibilities are clearly defined and communicated to all team members. This clarity can prevent a lot of misunderstandings and disputes.

3. **Encourage Collaboration:** Sometimes, conflict arises simply because team members are not used to working together. By encouraging collaboration through team-building activities or joint projects, you can help build rapport and understanding among team members.

4. **Conflict Mediation:** In cases where conflicts become more serious, it might be useful to have a neutral third party mediate the discussion. This can be someone from HR or an external consultant who specializes in conflict resolution. They can help facilitate a discussion that is fair and balanced, ensuring all parties are heard.

5. **Agree to Disagree:** Not all conflicts will end with a clear resolution, and that's okay. Sometimes, it's about reaching a compromise where each party agrees to disagree but respects the decision made for the benefit of the team and the project.

Implementing these strategies requires patience and consistency. Remember, the goal is not to eliminate all conflict but to manage it in a way that contributes to a more robust and cohesive team.

Maintaining Team Morale

After navigating through the choppy waters of conflict, maintaining team morale becomes crucial. How do you ensure that your team remains motivated and cohesive after a dispute? Here are some key approaches:

1. **Recognition and Acknowledgement:** After a conflict has been resolved, make it a point to acknowledge the efforts of those involved in finding a solution. Recognising their contribution to maintaining a harmonious workplace can greatly boost morale.

2. **Reaffirm Team Goals and Values:** Revisit and reaffirm the team's goals and values. This helps remind everyone of the bigger picture and the common objectives you share. It's a great way to realign the team and strengthen their commitment to the group's success.

3. **Foster a Positive Environment:** Work on building a positive work environment where positivity is as infectious as negativity can be. Celebrate small wins, provide constructive feedback, and encourage a culture of mutual respect and support.

4. **Provide Support:** Sometimes, conflicts can leave scars. Providing support, whether through counselling sessions or simply having an open door policy, can help team members feel valued and understood. This support system can be pivotal in maintaining high morale.

5. **Continuous Improvement:** Finally, treat every conflict as a learning opportunity. Gather insights from each incident and use them to improve your team's conflict resolution processes. This not only prevents future conflicts but also shows your team that their well-being is a priority.

By implementing these strategies, you can ensure that your team not only bounces back from conflicts but also grows stronger because of them. Remember, the goal is to build a team that is not just resilient but also feels empowered and valued.

Rewarding Excellence

Designing effective reward systems is a cornerstone for any entrepreneurial venture striving to cultivate a high-performance culture. The potency of your reward system lies not just in its ability to remunerate, but more critically, in its capacity to resonate with your team's intrinsic motivations and long-term career aspirations. To kick off, let's dive into the architecture of a reward system that aligns with both your business goals and your team's personal growth.

Firstly, consider the diversity in your team's preferences and the multiplicity of motivators beyond monetary compensation. Integrating a variety of rewards can cater to different desires and needs, such as professional development opportunities, flexible working conditions, or even wellness programmes. Such a system should ideally be transparent, where the criteria for rewards are clearly defined and communicated. This clarity not only helps in setting the right expectations but also ensures that the process is viewed as fair and meritorious by all team members.

Moreover, the timing of rewards plays a crucial role. Immediate recognition of achievements can have a more potent effect than delayed rewards. It reinforces the behaviours you want to promote almost instantaneously. Think about implementing peer-to-peer recognition platforms where team members can nominate colleagues for awards. These platforms can be incredible for morale and help foster a supportive team environment.

Next, we move on to recognising individual and team achievements. Individual recognition is straightforward – it's about acknowledging personal accomplishments, be it hitting a sales target or mastering a new technology. However, it's essential not to overlook the power of team recognition. Celebrating team milestones encourages collective effort and emphasises the importance of collaborative success over individual heroics.

When planning how to recognise these achievements, vary your approaches. Formal recognition can include award ceremonies or public commendations during team meetings. Informal recognition might be as simple as a thank-you note or a shout-out in a team chat. These gestures, regardless of their size, contribute to an atmosphere where team members feel genuinely valued for their contributions.

Encouragingly, technology can serve as a great ally in this domain. Utilise platforms that track and showcase team and individual achievements in real-time. These digital tools not only aid in maintaining a continuous loop of feedback but also help in keeping the team aligned with the company's goals and values.

Lastly, let's explore the realm of non-monetary rewards, which are becoming increasingly significant in the modern workplace. Non-monetary rewards can range from additional time off and flexible working hours to professional development and mentorship opportunities. These types of rewards can often be more cost-effective than monetary bonuses and have the added benefit of contributing to your team's growth and satisfaction.

For instance, offering a day off to attend a workshop or conference can be incredibly rewarding for an employee eager to grow their skill set. Alternatively, providing an afternoon off or a longer lunch break as a reward for team achievements can also be highly effective. These gestures show that you value your team's work-life balance and recognise their hard work in ways that contribute positively to their life outside of work.

Moreover, personalised rewards can significantly amplify their value. Pay attention to what motivates your team members individually. Some might value public recognition, while others might prefer private praise or a written note. Understanding these nuances can enhance the impact of your reward strategies.

In practice, implementing a thoughtful reward system requires constant iteration and feedback. It's a dynamic component of leadership that demands creativity and adaptability. Engage with your team regularly to gauge the effectiveness of your rewards and be open to evolving your strategies based on their feedback. This not only helps in fine-tuning the system but also reinforces to your team that their opinions are valued, thereby boosting morale and engagement.

In summary, crafting an effective reward system is not merely about giving out bonuses or gifts. It's about recognising and reinforcing the behaviours that drive your business forward. It's about showing appreciation in ways that resonate deeply with your team members, thereby fostering a culture of excellence and respect. By carefully designing, implementing, and continuously improving your reward strategies, you can significantly enhance team morale and performance, setting your business on a path to sustainable success.

RECAP AND ACTION ITEMS

You've just navigated through the crucial aspects of leading high-performance teams, covering everything from setting performance standards to designing reward systems that truly resonate with your team members. It's clear that managing a high-performing team isn't just about tracking metrics or resolving conflicts; it's about fostering an environment where excellence is recognised and rewarded.

Starting with performance metrics, you've learnt the importance of setting clear, achievable standards and the necessity of monitoring progress. Tools for measuring success are vital, not just for you, but for your team to understand where they stand and how they can improve.

Conflict resolution is perhaps one of the trickiest areas you will handle. Identifying the sources of conflict early and developing strategies to resolve them will help in maintaining a healthy team dynamic. Remember, the goal isn't just to quash disputes but to enhance understanding and cooperation among team members.

When it comes to rewarding excellence, the key takeaway is that recognition doesn't always need to be monetary. Non-monetary rewards like public acknowledgment, professional development opportunities, and additional responsibilities can be equally, if not more, motivating.

Now, it's time to put these insights into action:

1. **Review Your Current Metrics:** Take an afternoon to review the performance metrics you currently use. Are they comprehensive? Do they align with your business goals? Adjust them as necessary to ensure they are clear and motivating.

2. **Implement Regular Check-Ins:** Establish a routine of regular check-ins with your team. Use these meetings not only to monitor progress but also to catch potential conflicts before they escalate. This will help in maintaining an open line of communication and a positive team morale.

3. **Create a Recognition Calendar:** Schedule monthly sessions where team achievements and individual contributions are recognised. Make sure everyone in your team knows when these are happening and how they can contribute to these sessions.

4. **Experiment with Rewards:** If you haven't already, experiment with different types of rewards. Notice what makes your team tick. Sometimes, a simple 'thank you' note can be surprisingly effective.

5. **Solicit Feedback:** Finally, remember that the best way to improve is to learn from the source. Regularly ask for feedback from your team on these new systems and be ready to adapt based on their input.

By taking these steps, you're not just leading a team; you're empowering individuals and inspiring a collective drive towards success. Keep the momentum going, and remember that the strength of your leadership is reflected in the performance of your team.

ETHICAL LEADERSHIP AND CORPORATE RESPONSIBILITY

> "In looking for people to hire, look for three qualities: integrity, intelligence, and energy. And if they don't have the first, the other two will kill you." - Warren Buffett

Principles of Ethical Leadership

Delving into the principles of ethical leadership isn't just about ticking boxes for compliance or sprucing up your company's image; it's about setting the foundation for genuine, sustainable success. Ethical leadership is the backbone of a thriving business environment, and as an entrepreneur, mastering this can elevate your influence and legacy to new heights.

Understanding ethics in leadership

So, what does it truly mean to be an ethical leader? At its core, ethical leadership involves guiding your team and company with a set of moral values and principles. It's about making decisions that not only propel your business forward but also positively impact your employees, customers, and the wider community.

One might wonder, "Isn't that just good leadership?" Well, yes and no. Good leadership can drive a business to profitability, but ethical leadership ensures this profitability doesn't come at a moral cost. It's about long-term value over short-term gain. As a leader, every decision you make sends a ripple through your organisation, shaping the culture and setting the standard for what's acceptable and what's not.

The first step in understanding ethics in leadership is to define your core values. What do you stand for? Integrity, transparency, fairness? These aren't just fancy words to slap on your company's foyer. They need to be ingrained in your daily operations. From how you handle a contract to the way you respond to a customer complaint, these values should be visible.

You also need to be mindful of the ethical climate you're creating. This is the atmosphere of your organisation, and it's something that you control. Are you fostering an environment where team members feel safe to speak up about ethical concerns, or is there a veil of fear that covers wrongdoings? Remember, an ethical leader not only acts with integrity but also encourages it in others.

Consequences of unethical behaviour

Here's the kicker: unethical behaviour can dismantle the very fabric of your business. It's like a termite infestation eating away at your company's structure, often invisible until it's too late. The fallout from unethical decisions can be catastrophic – from legal repercussions and financial losses to irreparable damage to your brand's reputation.

Think about it. Companies caught in unethical scandals often find themselves splashed across headlines for all the wrong reasons. This kind of publicity can lead to lost customers, plummeting stock prices, and a toxic workplace environment. And recovering from this can be a Herculean task.

Moreover, there's a personal cost. Unethical behaviour can weigh heavily on your conscience. Sleepless nights, strained relationships, and a tarnished personal reputation are just the tip of the iceberg. As an entrepreneur, your personal brand is intertwined with your business. Any missteps in ethical judgement can reflect directly back on you.

To steer clear of these pitfalls, it's crucial to establish robust checks and balances. Regular audits, transparent policies, and a clear reporting system for unethical behaviour are essential tools in your arsenal. Encourage an open dialogue about ethics and lead by example. Show your team that ethical behaviour isn't just encouraged, it's expected.

Promoting ethical practices

Now, promoting ethical practices isn't just about avoiding the bad; it's about actively doing good. As a leader, you have the platform and the power to influence not just your organisation but your industry and community.

Start with training. Ethical training sessions, whether they're workshops, seminars, or e-learning modules, can be incredibly effective. They help clarify what's expected in terms of ethical behaviour and provide practical advice on handling ethical dilemmas. Make this training regular to keep ethics at the forefront of everyone's minds.

Next, lead by example. This can't be stressed enough. If you're preaching honesty but fudging numbers, your credibility flies out the window. Authenticity in your leadership style is non-negotiable. When your team sees you making tough decisions but holding firm to your ethical standards, they're more likely to emulate these behaviours.

Lastly, celebrate ethical behaviour. Recognise and reward employees who demonstrate strong ethical judgement. This not only reinforces positive behaviour but also signals to your team that ethical actions are valued and beneficial to their careers.

By instilling strong ethical practices in your business, you're not just setting up guardrails to prevent wrongdoing; you're creating a culture that thrives on doing right. This kind of environment attracts top talent, loyal customers, and, ultimately, drives sustainable success.

Embarking on this journey of ethical leadership is not just beneficial; it's essential for any visionary entrepreneur who aims to make a lasting impact. As you navigate through the complexities of running a business, keep these principles close. They will guide you, inspire you, and sometimes challenge you, but most importantly, they will help you lead beyond limits.

Social Responsibility

The Role of Businesses in Society

In today's world, the role of businesses extends far beyond the bottom line. As a business owner or entrepreneur, you're not just a part of the economy; you're part of the larger social fabric that binds communities together. Integrating social responsibility into your business strategy isn't just about doing good— it's about aligning your operations with the values and needs of the wider world around you.

Think of your business as a citizen of the world. Just like any citizen, it has rights and responsibilities. The right to trade and generate profit comes with the responsibility to contribute positively to society. This means considering the impact of your business decisions on various stakeholders, not just shareholders. It's about looking beyond profits to how you can contribute to the well-being of your community and environment.

For instance, consider how your business can help local economies. Can you source materials locally or provide jobs in underserved areas? What about offering your expertise to local educational programmes or engaging in partnerships that promote sustainable practices?

These actions help build a company that people respect and trust, which in turn can drive more sustainable profits. Remember, a business that only takes from its community without giving back is like a tree trying to grow in depleted soil—it may survive, but it won't thrive.

Implementing CSR Initiatives

Implementing Corporate Social Responsibility (CSR) initiatives can seem daunting, but it's about making a commitment and taking systematic steps towards realising it. Start by defining what social responsibility means for your company. Is it about environmental sustainability, community engagement, worker welfare, or perhaps all of these? Once you've defined your focus, you can begin to embed these principles into your company's operations and culture.

1. **Set Clear Goals:** What specific social outcomes does your business want to achieve? Goals might include reducing carbon emissions, improving employee satisfaction, or increasing community investments. Make these goals SMART – Specific, Measurable, Achievable, Relevant, and Time-bound.

2. **Engage Stakeholders:** CSR shouldn't be a siloed effort led only by top management; it requires engagement from all parts of your business. Furthermore, involve external stakeholders such as local communities, suppliers, and customers to gain different perspectives and build stronger, more meaningful initiatives.

3. **Allocate Resources:** Like any other aspect of your business, your CSR initiatives need funding, personnel, and time allocations to succeed. This might mean hiring dedicated staff, setting aside a portion of profits, or using a percentage of employee time for community service.

4. **Communication is Key:** Keep stakeholders informed about your CSR activities and progress. Regular updates, whether through social media, your company website, or direct emails, help keep your business accountable and demonstrate transparency.

5. **Monitor and Adapt:** Like any business strategy, CSR should be dynamic. Regularly review the impact of your initiatives against your goals. Are you

making the progress you hoped for? What can be improved? This not only ensures you're on track but also shows that your commitment to CSR is serious and not just a marketing gimmick.

Measuring the Impact of CSR

So, you've implemented a few CSR initiatives, but how do you know if they're actually making a difference? Measuring the impact of these initiatives is crucial, not just for internal knowledge and future planning but also for external credibility.

Start by revisiting the goals you set. For each, identify key performance indicators (KPIs) that can provide data on your progress. For example, if your goal is to reduce environmental impact, your KPIs might include metrics such as the amount of waste reduced or energy saved. If community engagement is your focus, look at indicators like the number of community projects supported or the amount of volunteer hours contributed by your staff.

Technological tools can aid in tracking these KPIs efficiently. Software that tracks resource use or analytics tools that measure engagement levels can provide real-time data that's invaluable for assessing impact.

Additionally, consider third-party audits or certifications. These not only provide an objective measure of your CSR performance but also enhance the credibility of your initiatives in the eyes of stakeholders and the public.

Finally, don't underestimate the power of storytelling. Share real-life stories about the impact of your CSR efforts—perhaps an employee who leads a volunteer project or a community that benefited from your support. These stories make your efforts relatable and tangible, showing that behind every statistic, there's a human story of change.

Incorporating CSR into your business isn't just a moral imperative—it's a strategic one. By taking responsibility for the social and environmental impacts of your operations, you're not just creating a better world; you're building a stronger, more sustainable business. So, take the leap, embed these practices into your company's DNA, and watch as you not only transform your business but also the society around you.

Creating a Legacy

Planning for Succession

Succession planning might not be the first thing on your mind when you're knee-deep in the day-to-day grind, but it's crucial for ensuring the longevity of your enterprise. Think of it as setting up a relay race where you ensure the next runner is as prepared as possible to take the baton and sprint forward.

First, identify the key roles in your organisation that are critical to its success. Who are your star players whose absence would be felt the most? Once these roles are identified, it's about looking within your team for individuals who embody the same ethos and possess the potential to fill these shoes. These are the people you want to invest in.

Developing internal talent not only boosts morale but also helps in retaining top talent. Provide mentoring, training, and gradually increase their responsibilities to prepare them for these key roles. Remember, effective leaders are made, not born, and your role is to craft a robust ladder for them to climb.

Moreover, communication during this process is vital. Be transparent with your team about your plans and how you envision the future of the company. This openness not only helps in smoothing the transition when the time comes but also aligns everyone towards a common goal.

Leaving a Lasting Impact

The mark you leave on the world isn't just about the profits you've made or the products you've launched; it's also about the impact you've had on people's lives and the environment. How can you embed a positive impact into the DNA of your business?

Start by thinking about the values that are most important to you and integrate these into your business operations. For instance, if sustainability is a key value, look at how you can make your operations more environmentally friendly. This could be anything from reducing waste, using sustainable materials, or investing in clean energy.

Next, consider the social impact of your business. This could be through creating inclusive employment opportunities, supporting local communities, or engaging in fair trade practices. Whatever your focus, the goal is to create a ripple effect of positive change that emanates from your business.

To truly embed this impact into your legacy, make these practices part of your brand story. Communicate your efforts and achievements not just as a marketing tool, but as a transparent report on your business's journey towards creating a positive impact. This not only builds trust with your customers but also inspires other businesses to follow suit.

Inspiring Future Generations

Finally, your legacy is also about the inspiration it offers to future generations. How can you ensure that your entrepreneurial spirit lives on and continues to ignite enthusiasm and passion in others?

One effective way is through sharing your story. Write about your journey, the challenges you faced, the mistakes you made, and how you overcame them. Make this narrative available – be it through a blog, a book, or speaking engagements. The more personal and honest your story, the more it will resonate with others.

Another approach is to engage directly with the next generation. This could be through mentorship programmes, workshops, or talks at educational institutions. These interactions not only provide you with a platform to share your knowledge but also allow you to directly inspire and influence budding entrepreneurs.

Moreover, consider setting up a foundation or a scholarship that supports young entrepreneurs who are looking to make a difference. Such initiatives not only aid in nurturing future talent but also ensure that your values and vision continue to influence long after you've stepped back.

In essence, creating a legacy is about looking beyond the immediate horizon and planning for a future where your business continues to thrive and contribute positively, even in your absence. Whether it's through meticulous succession planning, embedding lasting positive impacts in your business practices, or inspiring future generations, each step you take builds a bridge to a future that not only reflects your business acumen but also your commitment to making a difference. This holistic approach ensures that your legacy is not just remembered, but revered and continued.

RECAP AND ACTION ITEMS

You've just navigated through the crucial aspects of ethical leadership and corporate responsibility. From understanding ethics in leadership to measuring the impact of CSR and planning for succession, it's clear that these elements are not just nice-to-haves but necessities for sustainable business growth and societal impact.

Now, let's transform these insights into concrete actions that you can implement right away.

1. **Assess Your Current Ethical Framework:** Take a moment to reflect on your current leadership practices. Are they clearly communicated and consistently applied across your organisation? Start by conducting an audit of your existing policies and practices to see where you stand ethically.

2. **Develop a Code of Ethics:** If you haven't already, develop a robust code of ethics that outlines acceptable behaviours and decision-making processes. This will serve as a compass for you and your team, guiding everyone to make choices that align with your company's values.

3. **Train Your Team:** Organise training sessions that not only discuss what ethical practices are but also illustrate the real-world consequences of unethical behaviours. Use case studies relevant to your industry to make these sessions engaging and relatable.

4. **Implement CSR Strategically:** Identify key areas where your business can make a significant social impact. Don't just adopt CSR as a tick-box exercise. Make sure it aligns with your business values and integrates seamlessly with your core operations.

5. **Measure Impact:** Set up mechanisms to regularly assess the impact of your CSR initiatives. This isn't just about looking good on paper; it's about making a tangible difference. Use both qualitative and quantitative metrics to gauge your success.

6. **Plan for the Future:** Start thinking about your legacy now. How do you want to be remembered? Begin planning for succession early, involve your team, and ensure that the future leaders of your company embody the ethical standards you've set.

7. **Inspire by Example:** Lastly, remember that as a leader, your actions speak louder than your words. Be the embodiment of the ethics and values you preach. This authenticity will inspire your team, resonate with your customers, and

influence other entrepreneurs and business leaders.

By taking these steps, you not only fortify your own business against ethical pitfalls but also contribute positively to the broader business community and society. It's about setting a standard, leading with integrity, and leaving a legacy that inspires future generations to do the same. Let's lead beyond limits, not just in aspirations but in meaningful actions and enduring commitments.

OVERCOMING LEADERSHIP CHALLENGES

"Leadership is the art of getting someone else to do something you want done because he wants to do it." – Dwight D. Eisenhower

Handling Pressure and Stress

In the high-stakes game of entrepreneurship, pressure and stress come with the territory. You're constantly juggling decisions, managing teams, and striving to hit your next big goal. But here's the kicker: handling these pressures effectively is what separates top-performing leaders from the rest. Let's dive into some practical strategies to keep you functioning at your best.

Techniques for Managing Stress

First things first, managing stress isn't about eliminating it completely; it's about controlling it so that it doesn't control you. Here are some tactics that can help:

1. **Prioritisation and Delegation:** Begin each day by identifying the tasks that are crucial for your business's success. Use tools like the Eisenhower Box to differentiate between what's urgent and what's important. This simple tool can help you avoid the all-too-common trap of busywork. Once you've identified your priorities, delegate. Remember, delegation isn't about offloading work you don't enjoy, but rather about empowering your team and freeing yourself to focus on strategic decision-making.

2. **Mindfulness and Meditation:** These aren't just buzzwords; they are

powerful tools for managing stress. Even a few minutes of mindfulness meditation can decrease anxiety and increase your overall resilience. Apps like Headspace or Calm can guide you through short meditation exercises, which you can easily fit into your hectic schedule.

3. **Physical Exercise:** Never underestimate the power of physical activity in combating stress. Whether it's a quick jog, a session at the gym, or just a brisk walk during your lunch break, exercise produces endorphins—chemicals in the brain that act as natural painkillers and mood elevators.

Building Emotional Resilience

Emotional resilience is your ability to bounce back from setbacks and maintain balance amidst challenges. Here are some strategies to build your resilience:

1. **Acceptance:** Understand and accept that setbacks are part of the entrepreneurial journey. This mindset helps in managing your expectations and preparing you psychologically to face challenges head-on.

2. **Strong Support Network:** Build a strong network of friends, family, and professional contacts who understand what you're going through. Having people to talk to can make a significant difference in how you handle stress and recover from setbacks.

3. **Continuous Learning:** Adopt a growth mindset. View every challenge as an opportunity to learn and grow. This can be transformative, turning potentially negative experiences into positive drivers for personal and professional development.

4. **Voluntary Discomfort:** This might sound counterintuitive, but by regularly stepping out of your comfort zone and exposing yourself to controlled stress (like public speaking or networking in new groups), you can enhance your ability to handle stress. Think of it as stress inoculation—small doses can

make you immune to panic in high-stress situations.

Balancing Personal and Professional Life

Balancing the demands of your business with your personal life is crucial not just for your wellbeing, but also for your company's health. Here's how to maintain this balance:

1. **Set Boundaries:** This is crucial. Decide what hours you will dedicate to work and when you will switch off, and stick to these times as much as possible. Technology can help with this—use auto-responders to manage expectations about your availability.

2. **Quality Time Off:** Make your downtime count. Engage in activities that rejuvenate you and allow you to return to work energised. This might be a hobby, time with loved ones, or simply a day spent doing nothing.

3. **Reflection:** Regularly take time to reflect on your life's goals and evaluate if your current work-life balance aligns with these objectives. Adjust as necessary to ensure you're living a life congruent with your values and ambitions.

Incorporating these strategies into your daily routine will not only help you manage stress and build resilience but also ensure that you maintain a healthy balance between your personal life and your professional responsibilities. Remember, the goal is not to work yourself to the bone but to work smart and sustainably, ensuring longevity and success in your entrepreneurial ventures.

Overcoming Failure

Failure is an intrinsic part of the entrepreneurial journey. Embracing it, learning from it, and leveraging it as a springboard for growth can transform potential setbacks into powerful forwards momentum. Let's unravel how you can turn the tide on failure and make it work in your favour.

Learning from Failures

The first step in overcoming failure is to extract valuable lessons from it. This isn't just about acknowledging that something went wrong, but deeply understanding why it did. Start by distancing yourself from the immediate emotional impact of the failure. Treat it like a case study; dissect it objectively to uncover what can be learned.

Begin with the specifics: what exactly failed? Was it a product launch that didn't meet sales expectations? A marketing campaign that fell flat? Once identified, delve into the contributing factors. Was the research adequate? Were there missteps in execution? Understanding these elements can reveal insights that are crucial for your future strategies.

Next, engage your team in this learning process. Encourage an environment where honest feedback is valued over blame. This can be done through structured debriefing sessions where everyone is encouraged to share their perspective. Remember, diverse viewpoints can provide a more comprehensive understanding of what went wrong.

Documenting these lessons is just as important as learning them. Maintain a 'lessons learned' log that you and your team can refer to before initiating new projects. This practice not only prevents future mistakes but also helps in creating a culture that views failure as a stepping stone rather than a stumbling block.

Resilience in Facing Setbacks

Building resilience is key to not just surviving but thriving through failures. Resilience is about bouncing back stronger, and here's how you can cultivate it.

Firstly, maintain a growth mindset. Understand that skills and intelligence can be developed with effort, learning, and persistence. When you face setbacks, remind yourself that each is an opportunity to grow. This mindset will encourage you to take on challenges and treat failures as lessons rather than insurmountable barriers.

Secondly, resilience is built through small, consistent actions. Make it a habit to set daily or weekly personal and professional goals. Achieving these will build your confidence and reinforce the belief that progress is possible, despite setbacks.

It's also essential to manage your energy wisely. High-stress levels can erode resilience, making it harder to bounce back from failures. Incorporate regular breaks, physical activities, and hobbies into your routine to rejuvenate your mind and body.

Lastly, seek support when needed. This could be in the form of mentors, peers, or even professional help. Discussing your challenges and receiving guidance can not only provide emotional support but also offer practical solutions and perspectives that you might not have considered.

Creating a Supportive Environment for Risk-Taking

As a leader, fostering an environment that encourages calculated risk-taking can significantly impact how your team handles failure. Here's how you can create such a culture:

Start by defining clear values and principles that support risk-taking. Make it known that innovative ideas are welcome, even if they come with risks. Communicate that while not all risks will lead to success, all will be considered learning opportunities.

Encourage autonomy among your team members. Give them the freedom to make decisions and own their projects. Autonomy fosters investment in the outcomes, which in turn encourages taking thoughtful risks.

It's also important to recognise and reward risk-taking, regardless of the outcome. Celebrate the boldness of stepping out of comfort zones. When people feel acknowledged for being adventurous, they're more likely to embrace risk-taking as part of their professional behaviour.

Implementing a 'fail fast' philosophy can also be beneficial. This approach involves making small-scale experiments to test new ideas and iterate based on feedback. It reduces the cost and impact of failure and makes the idea of failing less daunting.

In conclusion, failure, when approached with the right mindset and strategies, can be a formidable tool in your entrepreneurial arsenal. By learning from failures, building resilience, and creating a supportive environment for risk-taking, you not only prepare yourself and your team to handle setbacks better but also set the stage for greater innovation and success in your entrepreneurial journey. Embrace these strategies, and watch how they transform challenges into stepping stones for success.

Navigating Power Dynamics

Understanding power within organisations is akin to learning the rules of a complex game. As a business leader, recognising the flows of power and influence within your organisation isn't just about climbing the corporate ladder—it's about making effective decisions that steer your company towards its goals. Power dynamics are the invisible forces that shape interactions and outcomes within your business. They can emerge from various sources such as roles, responsibilities, expertise, and personal influence.

To effectively navigate these waters, start by mapping out the formal and informal networks in your organisation. Who are the decision-makers? Who influences the decision-makers? What are the communication channels? Observing the patterns of interaction and decision-making processes will give you a clearer picture of the power landscape. This understanding enables you to engage more strategically with different stakeholders and leverage your influence where it counts the most.

Managing upwards and downwards

The art of managing upwards is often overlooked but is crucial for a leader. It involves managing your relationship with your bosses or board members. The key here is to understand their goals, pressures, and working styles. When you manage upwards effectively, you create opportunities to influence decisions and gain strong advocates for your projects and ideas.

Remember, managing upwards doesn't mean flattering your superiors or agreeing with them all the time. It's about being proactive in communicating, aligning your work with the broader organisational goals, and sometimes, having the courage to speak up when you foresee issues or better alternatives.

Conversely, managing downwards is about how you lead your teams. The cornerstone here is trust. Build genuine relationships with your team members. Understand their strengths, motivations, and career aspirations. Be transparent about your decisions and the organisational goals. When your team trusts your leadership and feels aligned with the vision, they are more likely to perform effectively and navigate through changes resiliently.

Effective management both upwards and downwards requires emotional intelligence, clear communication, and an ongoing commitment to personal and professional growth. As you grow in your role, continually reflect on and refine your management style.

Strategies for gaining influence

Influence in an organisational setting does not solely stem from the position one holds. It's also derived from personal credibility, expertise, and the ability to relate to others. Here are some strategies to help you build and exert influence effectively within your business:

1. **Build Credibility:** This comes from consistently demonstrating competence and integrity. Let your team and peers see that you are reliable, make data-driven decisions, and are accountable for your actions. Credibility makes people want to listen to you and follow your lead.

2. **Communicate Effectively:** Communication is not just about sharing information; it's about ensuring understanding. Tailor your communication style to your audience. Be clear about your ideas and why they matter. Listen actively to others' concerns and suggestions. Effective communication fosters collaboration and support for your initiatives.

3. **Network Strategically:** Networking isn't just for job seekers. As an entrepreneur, networking within and outside your organisation can amplify your influence. Engage with different departments, attend industry meetings, and connect with thought leaders. These relationships can provide you with insights, resources, and support when needed.

4. **Empower Others:** When you empower your colleagues and team members to succeed, you not only enhance their performance but also increase your influence. People support leaders who invest in their growth and value their contributions. Delegate meaningful tasks, provide constructive feedback, and celebrate their achievements.

5. **Adapt and Learn:** The business world is dynamic. Stay informed about industry trends and organisational changes. Adapt your strategies and learn new skills. A leader who is seen as a lifelong learner is more likely to be

respected and followed.

Navigating power dynamics is not about manipulating others but about understanding and engaging with the organisational forces in a way that is respectful and aimed at achieving the best outcomes for all stakeholders involved. As you enhance your understanding of these dynamics, and refine your approach to managing relationships and influence, you'll find yourself not just a participant in the game but a shaper of the game itself.

RECAP AND ACTION ITEMS

Navigating the turbulent waters of leadership isn't just about steering the ship; it's about being prepared to mend the sails and weather the storms. You've absorbed a wealth of strategies on how to handle pressure and stress, overcome failure, and effectively navigate power dynamics. Now, let's make this practical with actionable steps you can incorporate into your daily life as a visionary entrepreneur.

Firstly, dealing with pressure and stress requires a proactive approach. Start by integrating stress management techniques into your routine. Whether it's mindfulness meditation each morning, a weekly yoga class, or simply journaling your thoughts and concerns at the end of each day, find what resonates with you and stick with it. To build emotional resilience, challenge yourself regularly but constructively. Set small, achievable goals that stretch your comfort zones. Lastly, achieving a balance between your personal and professional life is crucial. This might mean setting clear boundaries about work times, or scheduling regular downtime or family days, which are non-negotiable.

When it comes to overcoming failure, remember that each setback is a stepping stone to greater understanding and improvement. Make it a habit to reflect on what didn't go as planned and why. Encourage an environment where your team feels safe to take calculated risks. This means celebrating the lessons learned from failures, not just the successes.

Regarding power dynamics, always stay aware of the undercurrents within your organisation. Foster open lines of communication and ensure you're as approachable to your frontline staff as you are to your management team. Managing both upwards and downwards with empathy and clarity will strengthen your leadership. To increase your influence, consistently demonstrate integrity, and be proactive in recognising and solving problems before they escalate.

Implement these steps, and you'll not only see improvements in your leadership but in your overall business health and workplace environment. Remember, leadership is a journey of continuous learning and adapting. Keep these tools at your disposal, and you'll lead not just effectively, but inspiringly.

THE FUTURE OF LEADERSHIP

"The greatest leader is not necessarily the one who does the greatest things. He is the one that gets the people to do the greatest things."
– Ronald Reagan

Emerging Leadership Trends

Latest Trends in Leadership Theory

In the whirlwind world of entrepreneurship, staying ahead isn't just about market knowledge; it's equally about evolving your leadership playbook. The latest buzz in leadership theory pivots sharply towards 'adaptive leadership'. This concept isn't entirely new, but its application is becoming increasingly critical as businesses face unprecedented changes. Adaptive leadership is all about mobilising people to tackle tough challenges and thrive in a rapidly changing environment. It encourages you to confront the status quo, question outdated methodologies, and embrace the discomfort of the unknown—all essential for a business aiming for innovation.

Moreover, the rise of 'servant leadership' marks a shift from the traditional command-and-control models to ones that emphasise serving the broader needs of others. Here, you focus on the growth and wellbeing of your teams and the communities to which you belong. This approach not only enhances team performance but also boosts employee engagement and loyalty. By prioritising the development of your people, you're building a resilient foundation that can weather any storm.

Another compelling trend is the integration of 'emotional intelligence' into leadership development. The ability to be cognisant of, control, and express one's emotions, and to handle interpersonal relationships judiciously and empathetically, is now seen as a cornerstone of effective leadership. It's no longer just about being smart; it's about being attuned to the emotional undercurrents of your team and harnessing that insight to drive productivity.

Impact of Technology on Leadership

Technology isn't just a tool; in many ways, it's now leading the charge, reshaping the very essence of leadership. The digital age demands a new breed of leaders—ones who are not only tech-savvy but also capable of steering their ship through the digital maelstrom.

Big Data and analytics, for instance, have moved from being mere buzzwords to essential instruments in decision-making. As a leader today, your ability to decipher vast amounts of data, extract actionable insights, and make informed decisions can set you apart from the competition. It's not just about having access to data but knowing what to do with it.

Artificial Intelligence (AI) is another frontier radically transforming leadership. AI's capabilities in pattern recognition, predictive analytics, and automated decision-making can significantly enhance efficiency and innovation. However, as you integrate AI into your business operations, your role as a leader must evolve. The challenge is to maintain a strategic oversight over AI, ensuring that it complements rather than replaces the human elements of your team.

Furthermore, the rise of remote working technologies during the global health crises has redefined workplace dynamics. Tools that facilitate remote collaboration and communication are now integral, urging you to lead teams you may never meet in person. The key here is to leverage technology to foster a sense of community, collaboration, and alignment with your organisation's goals.

Preparing for the Future Workplace

As you look towards the future, the workplace shows no signs of stability; rather, it promises continuous evolution. Preparing for this future means embracing a mindset of perpetual learning and flexibility. You might find yourself leading a workforce that spans multiple generations, with varying expectations and working styles. Understanding these nuances and adapting your leadership style accordingly can greatly enhance your effectiveness.

Moreover, the gig economy is on the rise, bringing with it a shift in traditional employment relationships. As a leader, preparing for a workplace that increasingly includes freelancers and contract workers means rethinking your approach to project management, communication, and team cohesion. It's about creating systems and cultures that support fluid, dynamic, and dispersed teams.

Another aspect of future-proofing your leadership style involves fostering a culture of innovation. Encourage risk-taking and offer robust support systems to help your team feel safe experimenting with new ideas. Remember, a culture that fears failure stifles innovation and ultimately hampers growth.

As you navigate these emerging trends, your ability to adapt and transform not only your business but also yourself as a leader, will define your success in the unpredictable world of entrepreneurship. By staying informed and proactive, you're not just surviving; you're thriving, ready to lead your team confidently into the future.

Leading in a Global Context

As you step onto the global stage, the complexities of leading in a diverse, international environment can be both exhilarating and daunting. The challenges are multifaceted, from navigating cultural nuances to managing teams that span continents and time zones. Here, we delve into what it takes to lead effectively in a global context, focusing on cross-cultural leadership challenges, essential global leadership competencies, and the intricacies of managing remote and diverse teams.

Cross-cultural leadership challenges

Leading a multicultural team requires more than just an understanding of different languages. It's about grasping the subtle cultural nuances that influence how people think, communicate, and react. For instance, while direct communication is valued in the U.S., in countries like Japan, indirect communication might be the norm where harmony and consensus are prioritised.

The first hurdle often involves communication barriers. Misunderstandings can arise not just from language differences but from the varied ways cultures express and interpret information. To lead effectively, you need to develop an acute awareness of these differences and adapt your communication style accordingly. This might mean learning to read between the lines in some cultures or being more explicit and detailed in your instructions in others.

Another significant challenge is decision-making. In some cultures, decisions are made top-down by senior leaders, while in others, consensus is key, requiring agreement from all involved before moving forward. Understanding these differences is crucial for you to foster a cohesive team dynamic and ensure everyone is on board with the direction you're steering the business.

Moreover, motivation varies widely across cultures. What incentivises a team in one part of the world might not work in another. For example, individual rewards are highly motivating in individualistic cultures like the United States, whereas, in more collectivist cultures such as China, group achievements and rewards might be more effective.

To navigate these challenges, it's essential to cultivate cultural intelligence - the capability to relate and work effectively across cultures. You'll find that being culturally aware and adaptable isn't just a nice-to-have, but a must-have in today's global business arena.

Global leadership competencies

In a world that's increasingly interconnected, certain competencies are pivotal for any entrepreneur aspiring to lead on a global scale. Foremost among these is agility. The ability to adapt strategies quickly in response to global market fluctuations is invaluable. This agility must be coupled with a vision that transcends local markets and taps into global trends.

Another critical competency is empathy. Understanding and genuinely relating to people from diverse backgrounds can help bridge the gap between different cultural perspectives and foster a more inclusive workplace. This goes beyond mere tolerance of differences to actively appreciating and leveraging these differences to enhance team performance and innovation.

Strategic thinking also plays a crucial role. Global leaders must be able to think several moves ahead, anticipating global trends and their potential impacts on their business. This involves a robust understanding of global economic, social, and political trends.

Furthermore, effective communication skills are indispensable. This includes not only adapting your communication style to different cultural contexts but also being proficient in using digital tools to communicate with teams across the globe. The ability to clearly articulate your vision and expectations, while being open to feedback from diverse team members, is crucial.

Lastly, integrity and ethical leadership are more important than ever. With businesses being held to high standards of corporate social responsibility, showing a commitment to ethical practices and sustainability can significantly enhance your reputation and influence on a global scale.

Managing remote and diverse teams

With the rise of remote working, managing teams that are not only culturally diverse but also geographically dispersed presents a unique set of challenges and opportunities. The key is to create a sense of unity and collaboration despite the physical distances.

Firstly, leveraging technology effectively is non-negotiable. Tools like video conferencing, real-time messaging apps, and project management software can help keep your team connected and ensure seamless communication It's also important to establish clear protocols for communication — for example regular check-ins and updates can help everyone stay on the same page

Building trust is another crucial element. This can be challenging when face-to-face interactions are limited. You might need to invest more time in one-on-one virtual meetings to get to know your team members personally and professionally. Encouraging open communication and showing genuine interest in their wellbeing can contribute significantly to building trust.

Furthermore, considering time zone differences is essential when scheduling meetings and setting deadlines. Flexibility might be required to accommodate various working hours, and being considerate of these differences can go a long way in maintaining team morale.

Lastly, promoting an inclusive culture is vital. Ensure that all team members, regardless of their location or cultural background, feel valued and included.

Celebrate diverse festivals, acknowledge different cultural practices, and encourage team members to share their backgrounds and experiences. This not only enriches the team's cultural tapestry but also enhances creative problem-solving and innovation.

Navigating the complexities of leading in a global context is no small feat. However, by cultivating the right competencies, embracing technology, and fostering an inclusive and adaptable corporate culture, you can lead your global team to new heights of success in the ever-evolving business landscape.

Sustainability and Leadership

Leading Towards Sustainability

In today's fast-evolving business landscape, sustainability is no longer a buzzword but a fundamental approach that can significantly propel your company forward. As a visionary entrepreneur, embracing sustainability isn't just about being environmentally conscious; it's a strategic pivot that enhances your brand, strengthens stakeholder relationships, and ensures long-term profitability.

The journey towards sustainable leadership starts with understanding your business's environmental impact and then seeking opportunities to minimise negative outcomes. This could mean adopting cleaner, more efficient processes, sourcing materials responsibly, or investing in green technologies. For instance, consider the surge in popularity of circular economy models, where products are designed and optimised for a cycle of disassembly and reuse. These models not only reduce waste but also open up new revenue streams and market opportunities.

Moreover, as a leader, your role involves embedding a sustainability mindset throughout your organisation. This means leading by example and fostering a culture where every team member feels responsible and empowered to act in environmentally friendly ways. Initiatives like regular sustainability training, employee-led resource conservation groups, and incentives for green ideas can cultivate this culture.

Remember, the shift to sustainable practices often requires an initial investment, but the ROI isn't just in dollars and cents. It includes enhanced corporate reputation, increased customer loyalty, and sometimes, compliance with regulatory requirements that could otherwise pose risks to your business.

Environmental Considerations for Businesses

Navigating the maze of environmental considerations can be daunting, but it's imperative for safeguarding your business against future risks. Climate change, resource scarcity, and stricter environmental regulations can significantly impact operational costs and market viability. Therefore, understanding these environmental factors and integrating them into your business strategy is crucial.

Begin by conducting a thorough environmental audit of your operations to pinpoint areas where your business has its most significant environmental impact. This assessment should cover everything from energy use and greenhouse gas emissions to water usage and waste management. Tools like the Global Reporting Initiative (GRI) can provide a framework for reporting on environmental, social, and corporate governance (ESG) performance, which can not only help you manage these impacts but also communicate them transparently to your stakeholders.

Adapting your business model to be more environmentally friendly could also open up new markets. For example, developing sustainable products or services can meet the growing consumer demand for green alternatives. Additionally, enhancing your company's operational efficiency through eco-friendly practices can reduce costs over time, thus boosting your competitive edge.

It's also wise to stay ahead of the curve by keeping abreast of environmental laws and regulations to ensure compliance. More importantly, proactive engagement in environmental issues can position your business as a leader in sustainability, earning you goodwill from consumers, partners, and governments alike.

Engaging Stakeholders in Sustainable Practices

The final piece of the sustainability puzzle is engaging your stakeholders – from employees and suppliers to customers and investors – in your sustainability efforts. Their involvement is critical because collective action can lead to significant environmental impact reductions.

Start with clear communication. Share your sustainability goals, strategies, and achievements with your stakeholders. Regular updates via email newsletters, social media, and annual reports can keep everyone informed and engaged. For instance, you could share success stories about how your company has reduced waste or highlight a new, eco-friendly product line.

Involving stakeholders in your sustainability initiatives can also take the form of collaborative projects. For example, you could work with suppliers to reduce packaging or partner with customers on a recycling initiative. These collaborations not only help achieve your sustainability goals but also strengthen your business relationships.

Moreover, consider the power of leveraging investor influence to drive environmental change. Increasingly, investors are looking to put their money into businesses that demonstrate a commitment to sustainability. By showcasing your sustainable practices, you can attract investment from these green-minded financial backers, which can provide the necessary capital to expand your sustainable initiatives.

In conclusion, integrating sustainability into your leadership style isn't just about making eco-friendly choices; it's about transforming those choices into business practices that ensure economic, social, and environmental health. As you continue to lead your business in these challenging times, remember that sustainability is not a destination but a journey of continuous improvement. By focusing on sustainable leadership, you're not just adapting to today's expectations but also setting up your business for success in a future where sustainability is expected to be even more central to business strategy.

RECAP AND ACTION ITEMS

As we've explored the dynamic realms of leadership, from emerging trends to global contexts and sustainable strategies, you've gained insights that are crucial for steering your business into the future. Embracing these concepts will not only enhance your leadership capabilities but also position your enterprise at the forefront of innovation and cultural sensitivity.

1. **Stay Informed and Adaptable:** The landscape of leadership continues to evolve rapidly, influenced significantly by technological advancements and new theoretical frameworks. Make it a habit to stay updated with the latest in leadership theories and tech innovations. Subscribing to relevant journals, attending webinars, and participating in think tanks can keep you on the cutting edge.

2. **Cultivate Cultural Intelligence:** As businesses become more global, understanding and integrating cross-cultural dynamics into your leadership style is more crucial than ever. Consider enrolling in cultural intelligence workshops or courses that can enhance your ability to manage and motivate a diverse, international team effectively.

3. **Embrace Remote Dynamics:** With the increasing shift towards remote work, refining your strategies for managing remote teams is vital. Invest in robust communication tools and technology that foster collaboration and connectivity, no matter where your team members are based.

4. **Lead Sustainably:** The push towards sustainability is not just a trend but a necessity. Begin by assessing how your business impacts the environment and identify areas where you can make significant changes. Whether it's reducing waste, using sustainable materials, or implementing energy-saving measures, small changes can lead to substantial outcomes.

5. **Engage Your Stakeholders:** Your journey towards sustainability will be more impactful when you engage your stakeholders in these practices. Organise workshops or seminars to educate them about the importance of sustainability and how they can contribute. Transparency about your goals and progress will also build trust and encourage a collaborative effort towards these shared goals.

By integrating these action steps, you're not just adapting to the future; you're actively shaping it. Leadership is not just about guiding others but continually evolving and setting new benchmarks. Your commitment to these principles will define your legacy as a forward-thinking leader. Let's lead beyond limits, inspire change, and transform our world for the better.

EMBRACING YOUR LEADERSHIP DESTINY

You have now travelled through a transformative journey exploring the multifaceted aspects of leadership. This exploration is not merely about accumulating knowledge; it's about fundamentally understanding your potential to influence, inspire, and innovate in any environment you find yourself.

Leadership is not confined to titles or positions. It is an aura that you carry that makes people gravitate towards you when they need direction, inspiration, or even a spark of motivation. You've uncovered the pillars of building a robust leadership foundation and the dynamism of strategic leadership. You understand now more than ever that leadership is about people—motivating them, inspiring them, and influencing them to achieve greater collective goals.

As you close this chapter of your learning, remember that the journey of self-improvement never truly ends. The landscape of leadership continually evolves, and so should you. Whether you are leading a small team or an entire organisation, the principles you've absorbed are the gears that will drive not just your success, but also the success of those around you.

The power of influence you wield is significant. It shapes not only your path but also the paths of others. It's a tool that, when used wisely, can forge destinies and sculpt futures. Thus, wielding this power with responsibility and integrity is paramount. As you inspire your teams, remember that their achievements are reflections of your guidance and vision.

Leadership also comes with its challenges—moments of uncertainty, decision-making in crises, and the continuous need for strategic adjustments. These are not just hurdles but opportunities. Each challenge is a stepping stone that tests your resilience and sharpens your leadership acumen.

Now, imagine a future where you are at the pinnacle of your leadership capability. You are not just functioning within a role, but transforming it. You have become a beacon of innovation and motivation that others look up to. This vision can be your reality. The tools and insights from this book are your blueprints; how you use them will define your journey ahead.

As you move forward, keep stoking the fires of your curiosity and commitment to growth. The landscape of leadership is vast and varied, and there are always new insights to gain and new horizons to explore. Your potential is limitless, and your capacity for impact is immense.

If you find yourself seeking further guidance as you apply these principles, remember that help is just a click away. Visit [WEBSITE LINK] to explore how professional insights can further tailor your path to leadership excellence. Whether it's refining your strategies, enhancing your influence, or continuing your personal development, the right support can amplify your efforts and accelerate your success.

Leadership is not just about what you do; it's about who you become in the process. It's about the values you embody and the standards you set for yourself and others. Your journey does not end here. Every day presents a new canvas on which to paint your leadership story. Every interaction is a chance to practice what you've learnt and to leave a mark.

Think of your leadership as a legacy—what do you want it to say about you? How do you want to be remembered by your peers, your team, and your community? These are not distant considerations but should be the core of your actions and decisions today.

As we conclude, let's revisit the essence of what it means to be a leader. It's about making a difference—one that is tangible and lasting. It's about elevating others as you climb and creating environments where others can thrive. Leadership is a journey of constant learning, of relentless pursuit of improvement, and most importantly, of significant impact.

Step forth with confidence and vigour. You are equipped, informed, and inspired. Your leadership journey continues beyond the pages of this book, in every decision you make, every relationship you nurture, and every goal you achieve.

The world awaits your leadership. Are you ready to embrace your destiny?

www.ingramcontent.com/pod-product-compliance
Lightning Source LLC
Chambersburg PA
CBHW050308230526
45471CB00005B/2080